Loving Relationships II

The Secrets of a
Great Relationship

Sondra Ray

creator of
The Loving Relationships Training

CELESTIALARTS

Berkeley, California

Portions from A Course in Miracles copyright © 1975 Foundation for Inner Peace. Reprinted by permission of the Foundation for Inner Peace. A Course in Miracles may be purchased from the Foundation for Inner Peace, P.O. Box 1104, Glen Ellen, CA 95442. The three-volume hardcover edition is $40. The single-volume (all-in-one) edition is $25 in softcover; $30 in hardcover.

Excerpt from Being, Evolution and Immortality (Wheaton, IL: Theosophical Publishing House) copyright © 1984 by Haridas Chaudhuri. Reprinted with permission of the publisher.

Excerpt from "Instead of Nagging — A Better Approach" from Glamour Magazine (May 1990) copyright © 1990 by Glamour Magazine. Reprinted by permission of the publisher.

Text design and typography by Jeff Brandenburg

Cover design by Sarah Levin

Cover art, "Two Hearts," copyright ©1988 by Beth Bonart

FIRST PRINTING 1992

Library of Congress Cataloging in Publication Data

Ray, Sondra.
    Loving relationships II / Sondra Ray.
        p.   cm.
    Includes bibliographical references.
    ISBN 0-89087-661-4
    1. Interpersonal relations. 2. Love. 3. Inner peace. I. Title. II. Title: Loving relationships 2. III. Title: Loving relationships two.
HM132.R29 1992
306.7—dc20   92-24732
                                                  CIP

3 4 5 6 7 8 9 — 02 01 00 99 98

Loving
Relationships II

I dedicate this book to every person I know.
Thank you for contributing to my life.

I dedicate this to every person I will know in the future.
Thank you for coming into my life.

—Sondra Ray

Prayer for this Book

Dear Babaji,

May everything I write be something beautiful for God.

May this book inspire us all to have Holy Relationships.

May it be a contribution to everlasting Joy and Peace all over the world.

Love,
Sondra!

Contents

Introduction

The mother of all personal growth seminars remains the maximum opportunity for a radiant new life. The Loving Relationships Training (LRT) is so deeply grounded in the timeless truths of ancient wisdom, it persists in being ahead of its time even in this, its third decade of serving a new age. Now, more than ever, as we move towards the turn of the century and the greatest transition in two thousand years, the message of Sondra Ray's remarkable blend of spiritual psychology, holistic healing, and common sense is both eminently practical and outrageously inspirational.

Sondra and I first met in 1977 when she, my wife Mallie and myself chose to combine our purpose to assist in the revelation of a passionate peace plan for the planet through the vehicle of individual loving relationships. Mallie and I lived on the East Coast, Sondra out West. She was from Iowa, Mallie from Vermont and I from NYC — all as different as day and night. We were inspired by Sondra's first book *I Deserve Love*; she was deeply connected to our unique coupledom. We all three were devoted to *A Course In Miracles*, which was coming into being around the corner from us in NYC. Moreover, Sondra was this amazing spiritual spark; Mallie this incredible environmental earth mother; I, this relic of the sixties, wanting to bridge living theatre, self-improvement, and political transformation.

All three of us knew something extraordinary was coming. We sensed that if we could find a collective sense of peace in the midst of the wild upheaval at hand ... if we could sustain loving relationships, stay on purpose, endure the turmoil, then anything was possible. We were all so deeply committed, so passionately devoted, so innocent, honest, vulnerable, and ultimately wise.

The years passed and we shared the vision with hundreds, thousands of students. Sondra had this unending energy, enabling her to plant seeds of immortality everywhere she travelled. Mallie and I brought the sense of family and the promise of a garden bearing fruit and fulfillment. Together, we farmed the planet: the new world and the old, the Middle East, and Down Under.

We rebirthed and rejuvenated. In NYC, LA, Seattle, SF; in London, Madrid, Stockholm, Paris, and Moscow; in Jerusalem, Auckland, Melbourne, Sydney, and Melbourne; in Mexico, India, Egypt, Greece, and Bali. We circled the globe with our constant message of love, truth, and simplicity; Sondra with the message of Babaji, Mallie and I with the very same message of family, devotion, divine motherlove, though sometimes seeming to come at the same conclusion from altogether different directions. Nevertheless, we all persisted through our differences towards our vision of the sweetness of unity spiced by the diversity of individuality.

We were all rebels in a way, yet committed to transcend our separation and find a field of unity, beyond competition and separation. In the best of families there are differences. This is the time to celebrate the differences, acknowledge the diversity, and inhale the blend of our unified purpose — loving relationships. Learning how to, not only live with the differences, but flourish by telling the truth fast and listening slowly, not being so eager to react, and respecting the truth of each part of the whole, yet seeking the highest thought, the one that serves the life urge the most.

Releasing the death urge, celebrating the gift of life, bathing in the sea of love, letting go of fear — Sondra Ray has been a guiding force, a full moon directing so many other guiding forces. She is the unseen hand, a magic wand of prayer, faith, and homespun wisdom. When she whirled into my life, I knew I was spinning in the right direction. I think you will too.

Don't be fooled by this being a sequel. *Loving Relationships* is still the spearhead of the future, the taste of a sweetness barely sensed.

In the twenty-first century books such as these will be acknowledged as handbooks for survival as well as undying torches to be passed on to future generations.

Love is a powerful, life-affirming force that flows through you when you surrender to it. This book is like a spiritual Hoover Dam. It spreads energy without draining the source; indeed, it replenishes the source by sharing so many of the secrets of love. Please, don't keep the secrets, pass them on. You deserve to love freely forever!

Bob Mandel
LRT International Director
Washington, Connecticut, USA
15th July 1992

· PART I ·

The Nature of Relationships

The Purpose of Life and Relationships

As a child, I was not at all certain of life's purpose. I searched for the answer in church sermons, my lessons at school, and the late-night conversations of grown-ups—all with limited success. In the end, I surmised that life's main purpose must be to forge a romantic partnership with another person. I was to find a man, give my love to him alone, have a family, and consider my task complete. These pursuits might have come very close to providing me with a satisfying answer. But content as I was, I could not rid myself of the idea that the purpose of our existence lay beyond this framework. And, secretly, I dreamed of being a missionary.

Eventually, I grew up and became a nurse, marrying immediately after college. Life seemed to be shaping up according to plan. Seven years later, however, my marriage ended in divorce. I was devastated and confused, my beliefs about the world shaken to their foundations. I had done all that church and society prescribed, but somehow the formula had failed. I found myself like a child again, with no idea of life's purpose.

It took me years to develop a deep understanding of this question—and my relationships did not really work until I did.

Every one of us is blessed with a higher self that has a specific life plan. If we make a personal relationship our main purpose in life, our sacred life plan may never be realized. With this vital impulse

3

squelched or diverted, we may find ourselves feeling lost, discontent and powerless. And it's hard to make any relationship work when we feel discouraged.

Remembering our purpose becomes part of the magic of self-discovery. And gradually the clarity we gain gives us the ability to:

- enjoy ourselves and life

- expand our creativity

- clear our karma

- perfect and heal ourselves

- make a contribution

- become enlightened

- find out who we are and express our divinity

If we are fortunate, our search for enlightenment may be made easier by a variety of tools and teachers, ranging from books we discover to inspired conversations with a friend, from the most ordinary experiences to the tutelage of living masters.

Throughout this book, I make frequent reference to *A Course in Miracles*, without a doubt the most important tool I have encountered. The Course is a three-volume set of books, an extraordinary manual designed to help change our perceptions about spirituality and the world we live in. The books explore the power of love as a guiding force in human actions and interactions. *A Course in Miracles* was taken down over a period of seven years by Dr. Helen Schucman, a highly respected research psychologist at the Columbia University School of Physicians and Surgeons. Schucman heard a voice dictating the text material to her—even as she fought its existence. Though nonreligious herself, Schucman believed the voice was that of Jesus. She committed herself to transcribing these fundamental teachings, assisted and supported throughout the entire project by Dr. William N. Thetford, head of the Psychology Department at the same institution. While *A Course in Miracles* has been extremely helpful for me on my personal journey, some of the ideas in this book are not consistent with the Course's teaching. Principles from the Course which I have used are clearly indicated and referenced.

A Course in Miracles calls the world a "teaching device (text, p. 74)," and the Course tells us that "the healing of God's Son is all the world is for (text, p. 476)." This is the sole purpose of our world's existence, and "thus the only one it has (text, p. 476)." If we recognize this truth, shouldn't every moment we live be directed toward the goal of healing and perfecting yourself, rather than aimlessly performing your daily activities without thinking? As the Indian spiritual teacher Krishnamurti has said: "Only those live who are really earnest, but the others fritter their life away and waste their existence."

While I am certain that you do *not* want to waste your existence, it is high time you wake up and discover who you are. For the more knowledgeable you become, the more you will be healed. Virginia Essene's *New Teachings for an Awakening Humanity* expands the discussion of life's purpose by describing our state of being:

> *We are light and energy because that is what god is. . . . We are ageless and eternal. We contain all of the truth you will ever need. We are here to demonstrate self mastery.*

Once we realize that we are *part* of, and not *separate* from God, we can begin to comprehend the *totality* of our being—and it is awesome. Because we create our own reality with our own thoughts, we are responsible for everything in our life. Understanding this truth, we become enlightened. Though I mention this in each of my books, *Drinking the Divine* is the one that can lead you to the deepest understanding of who you are. If you've made a serious commitment to search for the meaning of existence, I recommend you read the following books as well.

A Course in Miracles

New Teachings for an Awakening Humanity by Virginia Essene

Starseed Transmissions, Terra Christa and other works
   by Ken Carey

Cosmic Revelations by Ann Valentine

The works of David Spangler

The works of Robert Coon

Biographies and teachings of the masters of the Far East

These sources provide a wealth of valuable material for contemplation. In *Terra Christa, the Global Spiritual Awakening*, Ken Carey writes:

> *Each individual has a specific purpose for being on this earth. This purpose may contain numerous subpurposes. In the fallen state [believing we are separate from God] most people are only partially aligned with their life's purpose. They receive life energy only to the degree of their alignment. Overriding their life purposes, they remove themselves from the range of function where their energy is available; their vitality cannot help but diminish. Ultimately death is the penalty for persisting in such folly.*

When I visited India this year, one of my spiritual teachers, Shastriji, told me that I must remind people of the true purpose of life. "Many people just think about eating, sleeping, and having sex," he explained. "That is not much. Animals do that so that is nothing special. The real purpose of having a *human* body," he added emphatically, "is to recognize the Supreme." Think about this. As we acknowledge the Supreme, a new kind of life begins, a new kind of work begins. We become eager to share our joy with others.

"Love, Truth, Simplicity, and Service to Mankind: this is the formula for life," my Master, Babaji, used to tell us. Virginia Essene's *New Teachings for an Awakening Humanity* professes a similar truth—that the principles for right livelihood are Love, Purity of Thought, and Action. Indeed, if we do not follow these guidelines, we will suffer pain. Here, the concept of "action" means serving humankind *and* being responsible for the planet. How often do you remember that you are a caretaker of the planet? We have been given the gift of free will—to join together to build and create. But if we use free will in the wrong way—without love and wisdom, assaulting

Mother Earth—we only attack ourselves and create harmful karma, whose consequences we will later have to reckon with.

In our daily lives we must constantly work on our own purity, the integrity of our relationships, and our stewardship of the planet— always seeking a balance. Some people work on themselves a great deal. Forever occupied with their own enlightenment, they busy themselves with very self-involved tasks, making no contribution to the planet with the knowledge they have gained. Others are perpetually working to protect the planet. These people are often so busy "contributing" that they forget to work on themselves. Obviously, we must see to it that our personal concerns do not destroy our broader activities—and vice versa. We can and *must* rise above negative thinking and self-centeredness, creating peaceful relationships and acting as instruments of global peace.

Commitment to Purification

Great visionaries such as Jose Arguelles, who chronicled the Harmonic Convergence, warn us that we have only about 20 years to clean up our act. In his book, *Surfers of the Zuvuya*, José explains why the year 2012 is so crucial. He tells us that before that date we must become what he calls a "clean wave form." This means we let go of all old limitations, past life fears, ego trips, competition, control, and separateness. Those destructive patterns which limit our ability to love and create must be abolished. Once we've done so, people with clean wave forms will be able to make the best out of the chaotic situation ahead.

As we strive to develop a clean wave form, we will begin to discover our own individual and exceptional gifts. In case you feel uncertain whether you ought to invest your energy in this effort—let me be perfectly frank: discovering your particular path and contribution *is* your business on this earth. I recommend you keep asking yourself the following questions: "What am I doing to create a unified global civilization that is living in harmony with nature?" "How can I contribute to that goal?" "How can I inspire all the other people I know to work toward that goal?" Your answers lead us toward global unity, the precursor to universal peace and the key to our very survival.

I've stated that the totality of our being is awesome. But just *how* awesome? The Bible gave us a very clear indication of our potential and purpose here on Earth: "Be ye perfect even as God is Perfect." This is our assignment. Achieving complete inner mastery means that we become whole human beings striving for perfection in our *current form.*

Once we reach this level, we can aim for the next. We call this step *ascension*—a spiritualization process where even the physical body assumes qualities of the God within. During this process, the body's vibrations quicken until they merge with the inner light. Consequently, we are able to transcend death, dematerialize, and rematerialize. We can move from the early plane to a later one, coming and going. We can travel by thought, taking our body with us, or we can transform the body as we desire. Such are the abilities of a true spiritual master.

If, as Shastriji has said, the purpose of the human body is to recognize the Supreme, then we must also recognize that each of us *is the Supreme, along with everyone else.* Because each of us has the potential to become a Supreme Spiritual Master, this quest is therefore our destiny, the destiny of every soul. If we do not achieve this during this life, we will come back and keep trying. Ascension is in fact the culmination of many lifetimes of effort dedicated to spiritual attainment.

By achieving ascension—the Bible calls it "overcoming"—we must rise above ego delusions, disharmony, and death. Ruby Nelson's wonderful book, *The Door of Everything,* spells this idea out clearly. Nelson explains that if you have not handled your lower nature and death urges, your body will not tolerate the light vibrations of ascension. Physical immortality must be achieved before we can handle the light of dematerializing and rematerializing.

Discovering the purpose of your life *will* require your willingness to constantly change and improve yourself. You'll need to clear yourself through spiritual purification, to work out your karmic debts and to resolutely fulfill your own divine life plan. Making spiritual purification a regular practice in your life not only works, it gets you high. As you do these practices with another person, your relationships are filled with vitality and love.

Enlightenment

When we rescind our egos and dedicate our love to something greater than ourselves, relationships prosper. *A Course in Miracles* teaches us that we must *immediately* dedicate our relationships to the Holy Spirit if we want them to work (paraphrase, text, p. 337–338). When both people in a relationship truly know themselves as individuals, it is natural for them to want and create a holy relationship. When they commit to spiritual purification together as a way of life, the vitality and joy arising from their partnership is truly amazing. The union is strengthened when both partners are committed to holiness and service to humanity above all else. When the relationship is about supporting each other toward that purpose, the excitement of synergy and expansion surpass all boundaries.

Relationships teach us and force us to grow, expanding our identity outward. When partners follow the right track, they soon yearn to join together with other enlightened people, pooling their collective energies to make a real difference in the world. Once they team up with others, they will very likely want to create a "spiritual family" where everyone is working together sharing the light.

We in the Loving Relationships Training family invite you to be with us. We call our family the "Ohana," a Hawaiian word that means "extended family" or "family of people who breathe together." The LRT Ohana dedicates itself to the perfection of relationships and to life itself. It is a family committed to Peace. We have 14 centers around the world; in each one we try to help our members become all they can be. We accomplish this goal through everyday living, and through rebirthing and seminars that pass on the lessons we have learned.

Of course, many people have become enlightened without the help of seminars. As Terry Cole Whittaker, former Science of Mind minister, once said, "Life itself is an ashram and every moment is a spiritual opportunity." Many people have had their armor broken down by life's hard knocks and have become spiritually developed during the course of their trials. I have had both experiences. I've let life itself be my teacher, taking what comes, and I've consciously practiced spiritual purification techniques which break down the ego. I have found the second way faster and easier. I have listed the purification techniques I recommend in my book, *Pure Joy.*

The Eastern spiritualist Saibaba tells us that "the sole purpose of your incarnation is the crucifixion of the ego . . . to grow in love, to expand that love, and to merge with God and this is best done through service." I also like Ram Dass's ideas on this subject:

> *Why are you here? You are here to take the curriculum. You can use your own 'case' [your negativity, anger, lust, fear, and so on] as a stepping stone. . . . You move from somebodiness to nobodiness; when you are nobody you are free to be everybody and everything.*

All over the globe today, wondrous and unexpected discoveries about life's purpose are being brought to light by brilliant thinkers of our era. We would do well to keep abreast of them. Ken Carey, author of *Terra Christa, the Global Spiritual Awakening,* is one of these great thinkers. The profound significance of Carey's revelations has no limit. Example:

> *Never should an aspect of identity that perceived itself as separate from God dictate behavior.*

Think about it!

A Spirit of Peace in Your Relationships

I once lived with a man for just one day. He was quite wealthy and perhaps I was blinded by his riches and used poor discrimination. Anyway, I was not able to see the truth about the situation until we moved in together. As soon as we had all of our belongings unpacked, he began to pick a fight with me. I proceeded to tell him that I didn't do that (fight). This made him very angry. I told him I deserved peace and so did he. He stormed out of the house because he was so angry that I would not fight with him. He returned after one hour, having cooled off. He told me I was right, I did deserve peace, but that he could not live like that. I told him that I understood, and that we must end our living arrangement right now.

I was tempted to feel stupid and embarrassed; I could have easily beaten myself up for this mistake. Instead, I chose to point out to myself that at least I had caught the mistake in time and had the courage to go for peace. The writing was on the wall. In earlier days, I might have stayed and tried to negotiate. But now I knew the truth: he did not want peace. I confronted myself with the temptation of sex and money over peace and had to choose on the spot, and I did. This was not the time to worry about appearances or what my friends would say. It was time for me to get my head straight. He left and I was glad.

Problem Solving

Are you aware of the problem-solving dynamic that your family used while you were growing up? Who gave their power away to whom? Did your parents openly fight? Who usually won and how did he or she do this? Did the parent who was most angry make sure the other finally gave in? Did that person "stuff it all" and sulk? Did one parent storm out? Were conflicts actually resolved?

Think about your own problem-solving dynamics. Are you imitating your parents? What methods are *you* practicing?

Anger is hard on your body. The organs suffer and what is known as the etheric body takes a real beating. Anger also makes you age. During an argument, even when a very angry person "wins," she usually feels guilty afterwards, and the other is left withered and resentful. Either outcome drains us. Fighting is simply not an enlightened way of solving problems; it is a bad habit. Yet, perhaps because it is so commonplace, many still defend it, and there are many schools of thought that promote it.

People also have many excuses for defending and justifying anger. Often they righteously cling to it. *A Course in Miracles* states very clearly that anger can *never* be justified because "attack has *no* foundation (text, p. 593)." The first obstacle to peace, it adds, is "the desire to get rid of [peace]" (text, p. 380); in other words, the wish to be angry.

Although I have not always been able to maintain peace during every waking hour, this ideal *has* been and *remains* my goal. Since I committed myself to peace, I have only lived with men who share that ideal and are willing to stay with it. Of course, we are human beings, and temporary setbacks occur whenever we are processing the ego. These hitches, however, can be dealt with easily, once both parties agree that peace is their priority.

I have mentioned that there are those who find peace boring and believe life would be terribly dull without the "drama" of troubled relationships. I must simply ask these people, "Are you willing to see this differently?" All we have to do is tune in to the *spirit* of peace. When we do, all the glory of the Kingdom of Heaven opens to us. This joyous experience creates a passion so exhilarating that once you feel it, you will never wish to revert to conflictive behavior.

This spirit can only be felt when we rise above conflict and anger. For beneath every irritation, a well of hatred lies hidden. What's more, our job does not end with the elimination of external conflict and anger. We must deal firmly with internal conflict. In other words, we may not be openly fighting with our mate, but *in our own mind* we can still be in turmoil over our mate or with ourselves. Our own conflicting thoughts can keep us from finding peace, an attribute that we possess naturally.

Some people believe, in their struggle to be creative, that their trials and tribulations are necessary, if not desirable. They wrestle with the creative process and believe that hard times induce them to create. Little do they realize they might be able to produce beautiful and exciting works if they were free of constant struggle. The spirit of peace gives rise to tremendous creativity. It stimulates a natural, flowing creative process that requires no effort at all. When two people in a relationship simultaneously access this creative harmony, they experience an unimaginable thrill. The synergy combined within the magic of it all produces a near sexual experience. What potential we have! Why waste time diluting it with conflict?

Yet we can only mine these natural resources under favorable circumstances. When two opposing thought systems collide, it becomes impossible to attain peace of mind or peace in your relationships. We must choose one or the other: either the Holy Spirit's thought system, or the ego's. The ego's thought system—based on the idea that you are separate from God and all others—leads nowhere. It merely consists of a collection of all the negative thoughts we hold about life, ourselves, and other people. The ego's thought system leads us on a tour that passes from separation to fear, worry, depression, sickness, and death. As long as we indulge in such negative thinking and oppose the Holy Spirit's thought system, we confine ourselves to hell. Knowing we are one with God leads us to peace, abundance, health, and aliveness.

Because I knew there had to be a better alternative to arguing, I prayed for years for a way to prevent arguments. The simple technique which finally came to me gives us a way to train ourselves to turn matters over to the Holy Spirit. In the Loving Relationships Training we have transformed this technique into a kind of a game that helps prevent arguments. For it to succeed, both parties must be willing to play. (See p. 75-76.)

Before starting the game, each person reviews aloud how he's handled conflicts in the past. Did the method of conflict resolution work? Or did it end with one person manipulating the other? Did "resolution" mean that the "angriest" one took over, controlling and beating the other down emotionally? Did it amount to fighting the issue out until both people were exhausted? None of these methods bring satisfaction. They are destructive. We must be willing to look at the habits we've developed in the course of our relationships. Addiction to the old ways will prevent one from trying the new ones. After each person has evaluated the past, he or she must recognize the failure of old methods and agree to let them go. In this way, a space of openness is created, and new conflict resolution methods can arise.

Are you willing to find a better solution to problems than simply fighting?

I want to make it clear that I am *not* advising you to avoid expressing your feelings, for suppression is also very destructive to the body. Unpleasant feelings can tie you up in knots and cause disease; expressing these emotions diminishes their power over you. But expression is not an end in itself; the goal is to air your feelings and then *let them go*.

You can express your emotions without having screaming fits or huge, destructive fights. You can let your feelings be known in a way that is not harmful to you or others. Beginning with the words "I feel upset right now" works for me. After that, if I go on to share all my feelings, my discomfort can fade away. Because I use this technique, I know that I can create the space for someone to listen to me. I don't have to blow up. If the conflict centers around a very charged issue, I lie down and breathe out the emotions. Spiritual purification techniques show us that we can solve conflicts gently; we don't need to explode. This is why rebirthing is so effective.

In addition, once we realize that our disturbing feelings result from negative thinking, we have the power to transform those feelings by changing our thoughts. Expressing yourself fully must become a way of life. You have a right to express *all* of your feelings; when you value yourself, you realize that. The techniques that you find most useful are also those that benefit you most.

I am well aware that a number of contemporary self-help books actually *encourage* us to fight; I recently came across a guide whose author asserts that those who don't fight simply don't care about life! Such books not only advocate fighting, they also provide directions about how to fight "well." Within this context it is certainly true that not everyone in the world has learned how to deal with anger and *if* you *are* going to fight, you should not name-call and be abusive. But, how about a completely different tactic—making it your goal to *give up* anger instead of cultivating it? If you feel angry, why not work it out in ways other than yelling at your mate or family members? You can run around the block, scream in the shower or when driving alone in your car. At LRT, we recommend lying down and breathing out your tension and emotions on the exhales. Kicking your legs scissors style while breathing and keeping knees straight can also lessen tension. Perhaps you have developed your own techniques that help you cope with your anger in a positive way.

Comic behavior is another way of keeping an argument from building or stopping one. Did you know that some police officers are even taught to use comedy in their work? During their training, officers are sometimes taught to end domestic fights by acting in an unexpected or humorous manner. For instance, they may walk over to the refrigerator and help themselves to sandwich fixings! Because most of us are accustomed to very formal behavior from police officers, seeing one of them acting so casually is often such a shock to the battling partners that they often stop fighting right then and there. Our minds can create a myriad of helpful tools to diminish our rage. But the fundamental discipline we must master is the ability to let go of the negative thoughts that *cause* the anger. When you change these, anger will dissolve entirely.

People other than self-help book authors promote fighting as a helpful tool: even therapists have vehemently disagreed with me about the importance of letting go of anger. Sadly, some of them have wanted to fight with me about the issue of fighting! One in particular—a highly trained therapist from Switzerland—once gave me a long lecture defending anger. I let him express his opinion and decided to wait until after he attended our spiritual retreat to discuss the issue further. At the retreat, we all studied *A Course in Miracles* together, dividing the text in sections and teaching them to each other. As fate would have it, he happened to get a lesson that focused precisely on the subject of anger! He studied it with sincerity, and, in the end, I did not have to explain anything further. As his turn to speak arrived, he stood up in front of all the students, declaring humbly, "All my life I have defended anger. Now after reading this Course, I see that I was wrong." Shortly afterward he met and fell in love with his true soul mate, a woman who also happened to attend that retreat. And in the years following, he has gone on to defend peace, both personally and within his professional practice, based on that lesson he learned from the Course:

> *Anger always involves projection of separation, which must ultimately be accepted as one's own responsibility, rather than being blamed on others. Anger cannot occur unless you believe that you have been attacked and that attack is justified in return, and that you are in no way responsible for it. Given these wholly irrational premises, the equally irrational conclusion that a brother is worthy of attack rather than love must follow. You cannot be attacked, attack has no justification and you are responsible for what you believe (text, p. 84).*

Let's further explore just what occurs when we allow anger to overcome us. Psychologist Bonnie Jacobson has said that "yelling is a gesture of impotence." Among adults it causes rifts because it means you are not listening. Listening creates empathy, and empathy can create changes in behavior.

If you're intent on making these changes, Jacobson suggests that you first observe how you tense up when your mate says something that bothers you. After that, take a breath and "shelve" your anger for five minutes. The most important part of this process is to ask your partner questions about the angry statement he made so you can follow his line of reasoning. If, for example, he says, "I wish you didn't spend so much time with that friend of yours!" don't snap back. Try asking questions: "Oh, don't you like her?" Keep asking questions until something opens up. Try using your intuition to find out what is really behind this statement. For example, you might inquire, "Do you feel I spend too little time with you?" Even if the answer is no, he will appreciate that you are concerned. Tell him how you heard his statement, what you thought it meant. This way he can correct or confirm your understanding.

Let me say it once more: *keep listening and asking questions.* If you are addicted or even accustomed to anger, you may forget this infinitely important principle. And you must discipline yourself. You must also continually ask yourself, "Do I *really* want peace?"

In his book *Peace, Love and Healing,* cancer surgeon Bernie Segal provides a list of the "symptoms of inner peace,"composed by chiropractor Jeff Rockwell and his wife. With prolonged exposure, any one of us can eventually exhibit these "symptoms."

The Symptoms of Inner Peace

1. A tendency to think and act spontaneously rather than from fears based on past experiences.

2. An unmistakable ability to enjoy each moment.

3. A loss of interest in judging one's self.

4. A loss of interest in judging others.

5. A loss of interest in conflict.

6. A loss of interest in interpreting the actions of others.

7. A loss of ability to worry (this is a very serious symptom).

8. Frequent, overwhelming episodes of appreciation.

9. Contented feelings of connectedness with others and nature.

10. Frequent attacks of smiling through the eyes of the heart.

11. Increasing susceptibility to love extended by others as well as the uncontrollable urge to extend it.

12. An increasing tendency to let things happen rather than to make them happen.

If you have all or even most of the above symptoms, please be advised that your condition of *peace* may be so far advanced as to not be treatable.

Anger

Anger is very damaging to your etheric substances and organs. Anger should not be suppressed, but it does not have to be expressed either. My teacher Babaji said that all you need to do is change the thought that causes it. Are you willing to do that for the sake of your health? (We also recommend breathing out any heavy energy around it on the exhale during a rebirthing.)

I've been surprised at how many people would rather not hear this. They want to hang on to their anger because they are addicted to it (i.e., stubbornly *refusing* to get rid of it). They somehow feel powerful with it and of course defend it. Anger is the opposite of power. It is a sure sign of weakness.

Here is what some gurus have to say on the subject:

Guru Mai

It is said that if you are a true ascetic, you are completely devoid of anger. If there is any trace of anger in you, you are called a scoundrel, not an ascetic. A great being will go to any extent to remove the fire of anger. The greatness of a saddhu monk is that he can drop something once he realizes he has it.

Dalai Lama (from A Human Approach to World Peace)

We lose control of our mind through hatred and anger. If our minds are dominated by anger, we will lose the best part of human intelligence — wisdom. Anger is one of the most serious problems facing the world today.

Mata Amritanandamayi or The "Mother" (from Awaken Children!)

Anger and impatience will always cause problems. Suppose you have a weakness of getting angry easily. Once you become normal again, go and sit in the family shrine room or in solitude and regret and repent your own anger and sincerely pray to your beloved deity or Mother Nature, seeking help to get rid of it. *Try to make your own mind aware of the bad outcome of anger.* When you are angry at someone, you lose all your mental balance. Your discriminative power completely stops functioning. You say whatever comes into your mind and act accordingly. You may even utter crude words.

By acting and thinking with anger you lose a lot of good energy. Become aware that these negative feelings will only pave the way for your own *destruction*.

Forgiveness

Catherine Ponder has written much about the subject of forgiveness and health. She says, "Resentment, condemnation, anger, the desire to get even or to see someone punished or hurt, are thoughts that rot your soul and tear down your health. You must forgive for your own sake. All illness will not be fully healed while you continue to remain unforgiving." You must constantly forgive, she says, in order to be healthy and happy. She goes so far as to say that "If you have a problem, you have something to forgive . . ." and forgiveness will unblock whatever it is that stands between you and your god. She offers this affirmation in her book *The Dynamic Laws of Healing* (which I definitely recommend):

> *All that has offended me, I forgive. Whatever has made me bitter, resentful, unhappy, I forgive. Within me and without, I forgive. Things past, things present, things future, I forgive.*

When you have a hard time forgiving, you might ask yourself: Why am I refusing to forgive? Why am I afraid to forgive? Why am I unwilling to see that I created this situation? (There are no victims.) Why did I need that situation in my life?

PRAYER

May I abandon the Anger Habit.

O Eternal Tranquility!
Save me from attacks of fury fever
that shock my nerves and inflame my brain.

May I abandon the anger habit
that brings unhappiness to me and my companions.
Let me not indulge in fits of selfish vexation
that alienate from me the affection of my loved ones.

May I never invigorate my resentments
by attentively refueling their fires.

O Queen of Quietude!
Whenever I am rageful place thou before me a chastening mirror
in which to see myself made ugly by passion.
Let me not appear disfigured before others,
my face wrath-wrecked.

I would solve the difficulties of life through
thoughts and acts of love, not of hate.
Bless me, that I heal anger hurts in myself
with the salve of self-respect
and anger hurts in others with the balsam of kindness.

May I realize, O SPIRIT,
that even my worst enemy is still my brother,
and that, even as thou lovest me, thou lovest him.

Yogananda

Anger Is Never Justified
A Course In Miracles

Review

Purpose of Life and Relationships

1. Get clear on your purpose in life.

2. Work toward making a contribution.

3. Find out who you are and what it means to be one with God.

4. Remember that life is a school and you must always be a student who strives for excellence.

5. Perfect yourself.

6. Continually expand your creativity.

7. Heal yourself of your ailments and hang-ups. Clear yourself continually.

8. Remember that you are responsible for your own thoughts, and that thoughts produce results—always think positively.

9. Recognize that you are light and energy and so is everyone else.

10. Always enjoy yourself, knowing that God's will for you is perfect happiness.

11. Live by these principles: love, truth, simplicity, purity of thought and action, and service to humanity.

12. Become responsible for conditions on the planet. Be a caretaker of Mother Earth.

Purification and Enlightenment

1. Along with your partner, dedicate your relationship to something greater than both of you.

2. Always pursue a Holy relationship, committing to holiness above all else.

3. Do spiritual purification techniques together with your mate regularly.

4. Make it your purpose to become a "superbeing." Transform your relationship into a sacred space where that can happen.

5. Become part of a spiritual family that helps you progress. Join with others.

6. Balance work on yourself with efforts to serve humanity and the planet.

The Spirit of Peace

1. Make peace your goal.

2. Become aware of the dynamic for problem solving that existed in your family when you grew up.

3. Realize that the ego loves conflict and that the first obstacle to peace is the desire to get rid of peace itself—be vigilant.

4. Do not defend anger.

5. Give up all the "battles" in your mind, one by one.

6. Always try to prevent arguments.

7. When you feel criticized, before getting angry or upset, take a breath, ask questions of the meaning of the feedback. Listen, don't yell.

8. Train yourself to use the Holy Spirit's thought system instead of the ego's.

9. Turn over all your problems to the Holy Spirit, as only the Holy Spirit is conflict free.

What To Do During an Anger Attack

1. Do not yell at anyone else.

2. Lie down and breathe, pumping out the anger on the exhale. (It helps to know the rebirthing breath.)

3. If that doesn't work, run around the block until calm.

4. When you calm down, remind yourself of these two verses from *A Course in Miracles*:

    a) *You will attack what does not satisfy you to avoid seeing that you created it.*

    b) *Beware of the temptation to perceive yourself as unjustly treated.*

5. This means you created the result you are angry at. You somehow needed it, so try to get enlightened fast and see your part. (What is your payoff?)

6. Express yourself now sanely:

    "I felt angry because _____."

    "I see I had this thought _____ that attracted this situation."

7. Do the above process recommended by the "Mother."

8. Write down all your feelings of anger — then burn them.

9. Call a friend who is enlightened and more sane than you right now to get processed.

10. Do a truth process:

    "The reason I do not want to forgive _____ is _____."

11. Remember that forgiveness is the key to happiness and health. When you are sick, there is usually someone you have not forgiven.

12. Remember: *Behind every grievance is a miracle.*

13. Remember anger is one of the causes of aging and death. It's *not worth it.*

· PART II ·

Another Look at Relationships

Meeting and Mating

The soul draws toward itself the circumstances and people it needs for its highest development. In the same way, our karma and vibrational patterns draw us to the very person we need to help us grow.

In all our personal interactions, we must help each other develop love and kindness. A personal relationship is a sacred responsibility—it should not be based on physical, intellectual, or emotional attraction alone. Such a partnership must be based on a commitment to manifest the highest and best in one another.

Conception Trauma and Relationships

The last decade and a half have given birth to investigations that chart the origins of our attractions to, and relations with, other people. Among the startling findings: the way we meet, enter, or begin a relationship may be related to our own conception in our mother's womb. Having an understanding of the circumstances surrounding how you were conceived will help to make the conception of your relationships more conscious. The following example—seemingly far-fetched but actually quite commonplace—illustrates this phenomenon: A male baby is conceived accidentally, the pregnancy unwanted by his parents. As a young adult, the former unwanted child finds himself attracted to women who do not really want to commit to a relationship; he becomes very emotionally involved in them anyway. A woman may even overtly reject him, but he keeps trying to maintain a bond. Perhaps he finds himself with women who may even date him, but reject him sexually. Either way, he ends up feeling "unwanted." These will be very unsatisfying relationships right from the start, yet he is "hooked" on unrequited love. Why? Because he has the unconscious need to recreate the feeling of being unwanted, since that is what he is accustomed to.

If your conception was an "accident," you may just find yourself time and time again stumbling into relationships unconsciously, then suddenly waking up and wondering how you became entangled. This may occur because you are continually meeting partners under circumstances that not only mirror your own conception, they may also resemble your birth. I was able to identify this dynamic in my own life: I was born on the kitchen table, and for many years I would either meet men in restaurants or go out with restaurateurs!

The more we are conscious of these dynamics in our personal relationships, the more freedom we will have to pick and choose partnerships that will work in our favor. As you can see, unsolved conception trauma can cause pain both to ourselves and to other people with whom we mate. If we remain unaware of how the conception experience affects our decisions and actions, we give up a great deal of power over our lives.

Dismal as it may seem, "I don't want to be here" is a sentiment felt by a substantial number of people. These individuals could have adopted such anti-life feelings early on—either just before or immediately after their own birth—if they did not like being taken from or being in the womb. If they had a rough time coming out into the world, they may have decided that they "don't want to be here" during the birth trauma. You would be well advised to keep this phenomenon in mind, especially if you find your new relationship taking the following course: You meet a person, and you're very attracted to them. The attraction seems to be mutual, but before you know it, they are avoiding you and don't want to be in the relationship. They may like you very much, and even flirt with you, but the relationship never gets off the ground. The only reason that they give is that they simply "don't want to be here." Though such people occasionally do make it through the initial meeting phase and actually enter into relationships, nine times out of ten, they are not totally "there." They're unable to be present for their partner or themselves: consciously or unconsciously, they are obsessed with the need to leave.

To understand more about how conception, pregnancy, and birth affect relationships, I refer you to the book I co-authored with Bob Mandel, *Birth and Relationships*, which is a comprehensive overview of this new and important area of research.

Relationship Phases and Adjustments

In an excellent article published in Australia's *Intent* magazine, Rob Tillet writes:

> When our attention is aroused by the presence of another energy field from another person, our chakras attempt to make a contact with this new field by preparing to receive and transmit energies. We are surrounded by an energy field that can occupy quite a space around our physical form. We are actually swimming in a field of energies.
>
> The essential nature of a relationship is energy exchange. When we meet a person for the first time, we are either attracted, repelled, or indifferent to him or her . . . according to the way in which an energy connection is established. Relationships consist of the exchange and mutual processing of energies. A healthy relationship is one in which the energy exchange is mutually beneficial to the participants. That would be called a *strengthening relationship*: one in which both of the partners are stronger as a result of the relationship than they would be without it. A *weakening relationship* is one in which the energy exchange is actually destructive to the health and well being of the partners.
>
> When we form any kind of relationship, our chakras seek to connect with the appropriate chakra of the other person. When

all chakras connect at the appropriate frequency, a dyadic, or totally fulfilling relationship develops.

In my book *Loving Relationships I*, I talked about how to create mates in your life. In this sequel I would like to make a more in-depth investigation into the reasons why we attract the people we attract. *The Esoteric Philosophy of Love and Marriage,* by Dion Fortune, has the best explanation that I have found, and I recommend you study this book carefully. Dion Fortune states that souls can couple in three different ways:

• Through ordinary attractions of sex

• By renewing karmic ties

• According to higher cosmic laws

The Sexual Tie: Unfortunately, many people hurry into a permanent mating, urged on by physical desire. They may then resort to marriage with the first available partner. Often, they will erroneously rationalize their feelings by idealizing the object of their desire. Suddenly one day they realize they have bound themselves for life to a person who is incapable of satisfying any of their needs. Misery follows. This is a very important point: one's judgment can cloud over completely when blinded by sexual desire.

The Karmic Tie: Bonds based on karma are less easy to distinguish. Karmic ties are rooted in attractions experienced in past lives. For a full discussion of this phenomenon, I recommend you read the book *We Were Born Again to Be Together* by Dick Supter for further information, and also *Other Lives, Other Selves* by Roger Woolger.

The Cosmic Tie: This is the most profound and potent tie. It is a partnership entered into by two individuals for the sole purpose of performing a special service; it is motivated by service alone. The partners in this union do not choose each other. They offer themselves for service to the Master on the Inner Planes. They are mated with attention to their qualities and capacities. The pair opens a channel. Divine forces flow through them with astounding power, magnetizing them and their surroundings. Through this union, the power of each partner is augmented; they are brought to their highest level of perfection.

After describing the different types of unions, Dion Fortune talks about the importance of mating on *matching planes*. The first plane is the physical and material, the second plane is the lower astral, the third plane is the upper astral, the fourth plane is the lower mental, the fifth plane is the upper mental, the sixth plane is the lower spiritual, and the seventh plane is the upper spiritual. According to Fortune, unless we mate on each one of our planes, our union will be incomplete. For instance, if a man who has three developed planes marries a woman who has but two that are functioning, psychic and spiritual disaster can occur. Due to their negative effect on these inner planes, promiscuous sexual relations are not taken lightly.

Fortune advises us that before we mate seriously, we should contact a very reliable psychic and astrologer. She believes that we should take time before marrying, so that we have a chance to discover whether the relationship strengthens or weakens us. In a perfect marriage, Fortune writes, "the pair mate with each higher plane as it comes into function, applied to evolution: these two enter into the light." Thank you, Dion. (Read her books!)

An ideal union, of course, will often require a lengthy journey. As we make our way through the initial stage of a relationship—its conception—we must keep in mind that a new relationship means a *big change*. On the surface, this idea may seem obvious. But the fact that transitions tend to activate *birth trauma memories* is not so readily apparent. Tension rooted in these very early memories, may mount very soon after your new relationship begins. The LRT adage, "Love brings up anything unlike itself," reveals another reason interactions soon become rocky. In practical terms, this means that your mate's love, which is a kind of energy, will purge you of anything unlike love—including guilt, fear, pain, doubt, the death urge, and so on. We might compare this to trying to clean out a glass of water that has a layer of sediment on the bottom of it. As you pour in more water, the mud gets stirred up. The unexpected appearance of negative feelings—just when we think we have finally found a safe and loving relationship—may be very, very confusing. It will be important to know in advance, therefore, that the sudden appearance of negative feelings may indicate healing—not disintegration. It helps a great deal to have techniques like rebirthing to help you get through these phases of adjustment.

Patterns

When a couple survives the initial highs and lows of a budding relationship, they may consider making a commitment. If both want to be fully committed at the same time in the same degree of intensity, this stage can be very exciting. Often, however, a clumsy dance occurs in which one partner is more strongly committed, the other less so: the old story of "when I want you, you don't want me. So I back off and don't want you and then you want me." Some people get through this and some don't. It can be quite maddening, to say the least.

It is also important to understand that this is a *pattern*. A pattern is what we call "Repetitive Unconscious Behavior." Patterns are often based on repetitive behaviors in our blood families or reactions to those behaviors. In the Loving Relationships Training we discuss patterns in relationships; some of these are also described in *Loving Relationships I*.

What motivates us to want someone obsessively when feelings of affection are not mutual—or vice versa? In examining cases like these, what we at LRT call the "incest taboo pattern," can usually be found. This frustrating pattern begins during childhood. If you are female, you could not have your father, the man you really wanted. The way in which you cope with this disappointment is decided very early—and its effects continue into adult life. As an adult, when you can't have the one you really want because you have set him up as your father (or vice versa with the mother), that relationship then becomes "taboo" also.

This is a very deep and complex pattern. It often takes people many years to work it out. If we manage to suppress it enough in the beginning stages of the relationship, we may actually make a commitment, and move in with or even marry a partner. But the incest taboo pattern, based as it is on such a powerful impulse, usually surfaces sooner or later. The results can surprise and bewilder us. Some people actually find out that the minute they get married, sex no longer provides enjoyment or pleasure; others quickly disappear from the relationship altogether.

A relationship can generate a fantastic amount of energy when partners feel equal passion for one another. Yet maintaining an even balance is quite challenging. As I explained before, "love brings up anything unlike itself," and passionate love frequently stimulates too many unconscious negative thoughts at once. A couple may become very happy, high, and passionate for days—then something inexplicable happens between them and suddenly the feelings disappear or go away. Because of the negative subconscious thoughts that have surfaced, partners need to know that this loss of passion is *natural* and *temporary.* Whenever it occurs, it's time to clear or process, and practice spiritual purification. At LRT, we would say that the couple's "case came up." This means that the partners' birth trauma got activated, their unconscious death urge was stimulated, and their negative thought structures or family patterns surfaced. The tremendous love energy then produced pushed all these latent impulses outward. It is important not to get angry and give up at this time if you want to stay in this relationship. However, at this point, people often get disillusioned with each other, blaming each other for a waning romance. Ironically, this is just the moment when it is so crucial to have faith in yourself and your partner. It is a time to fortify the relationship with an enlightened understanding of how the mind works and a knowledge of spiritual purification. If a couple gets rebirthed at this time, they can breathe out the subconscious material that has surfaced and then go back to the love quite easily.

A crisis in your relationship can also provide an opportunity to develop a deep and mature love. This kind of bond celebrates our humanity—including our imperfections. By contrast, an immature love requires constant novelty; when the novelty declines, a new attraction is sought. Immature love needs a perfect idol as a love object. Lacking integrity, this kind of bond is frail and often shallow. But in a *mature love*—a relationship between two spiritual beings— a couple has the ability to weather love's unpredictable changes.

Though partners brought together by an immature love may, by some accident, make it through the initial phases of a relationship, they will have unconsciously established destructive methods of problem solving. Unfortunately, the practice of fighting or "stuffing it" figures prominently among them. This damaging behavior can be habit forming, dragging on for years and years until fighting leads to separation or "stuffing" the anger causes pain and disease.

I can't emphasize how crucial it is for couples to develop spiritually enlightened methods of problem solving and clearing during these early stages of a relationship. Right from the beginning you'll need to discuss basic questions such as your purpose in life, your purpose in the relationship, what techniques you use to clear yourself and how each of you can serve the other. Some people don't talk about these things until it is too late; bad habits have already formed. That's why honest discussion must begin immediately. By talking about these things from the start, you can also determine whether this new person will blend with your life style and spiritual goals. If your partner cannot handle this kind of discussion at all, consider this behavior as a sort of a "red flag" warning. You may not want to pursue a deep emotional relationship with that individual. Remember, there are people who not only tolerate, but require honest dialogue. Isn't this what you deserve? Seek them out!

Intimacy

When you *do* find someone with real potential as a mature lover, set to work together envisioning what your relationship will look like. In this early stage you may need to negotiate what we in the Loving Relationships Training call "the game." The "loving" aspect of your loving relationship is already handled: you are love and the other person is love, too. All you need to do is keep removing the blocks preventing the awareness of love's existence. But the "relating" aspect of your partnership is where "the game" comes in. It works like this: you invent and try out a game such as "Let's move in together and be monogamous," or, "Let's be monogamous but live apart," or, "Let's date and see each other three times a week," or "Let's just be friends and wait a few months before we sleep together." Once you both agree on a game plan, try it out in practice and see if you align. If the game you've chosen doesn't quite work, renegotiate. Remember, *it's important not to impose the exact form or pacing from a previous partnership on your new one.* Each new person has a unique history and birth, unique patterns, fears, and desires. You must compose a new dance, a synthesis of your partner and yourself. This poses a real challenge, but it can also be some of the most fun you've ever had.

Satisfying individual needs is part of the answer, but there are other aspects of relating that may need your attention as well. Deep intimacy itself can be rather frightening. This does not mean you will always be aware of your fear—it may be suppressed. What you *will* notice is that one or both of you suddenly pull away, or become constantly distracted, or submerged in work activities. Before you know it, you and your mate are rarely seeing each other. A pattern develops in which you have your own separate worlds. Such alienation often indicates an avoidance of intimacy or fear of facing subconscious material that may surface if you really got close to someone.

On the other end of the intimacy spectrum, you may find yourselves spending *too much* time together, so that you end up smothering each other—unintentionally contributing to a loss of self. To catch them in time, each partner must be aware of these tendencies. Rather than running away, each person must be aware of his or her own behavior patterns, and face them head-on.

To begin to understand the way patterns affect our lives, I recommend you slowly and carefully read the following profile, drawing parallels to similar examples you know of.

> A small girl's father leaves the family when she is three years old. Because the chid is very young, she appears largely unaffected. As an adult woman, she may attract a man who has a pattern of leaving partners. It is very likely that this man learned to leave as a survival mechanism in his own early childhood. Perhaps as he tried to enter the world, he got stuck in the womb. Deep in his psyche, the thought "I have to get out in order to survive," took hold.

When the man and woman in question meet, it is love at first sight; perhaps they both love cooking and dancing, skiing and poetry. Though it would appear that they are attracted to one another by common interests, in fact, it is their unconscious patterns that have actually attracted them to one another. How long will the marriage last? Perhaps *three years*. This woman may or may not realize that this was her age at the time her father left. But as her partner leaves, she cries, reinforcing her childhood conviction that "men leave me." And here is the crux of the matter: if she does not change that conviction, she will probably recreate it again and again in her future relationships.

I have asked my colleague, Rhonda Levand, to expand this discussion with an essay on patterns, sexuality and how the LRT helps us to change them:

Sex Gets Better After Taking the Loving Relationships Training

by Rhonda Levand

In 1981, I decided to take the Loving Relationships Training. A healthy woman in my thirties, I'd been married for eight years and had had numerous sexual experiences, and yet I'd never really enjoyed sex. I had often disappointed my partners sexually—and I had never had an orgasm.

After completing the Loving Relationships Training, I began to really enjoy sex, finally relaxing enough to have orgasms. During the course of the training, I came to realize that sexuality was the key issue I had to heal in my own life. My parents, especially my father, had wanted a son, not a daughter. His disappointment registered clearly in my mind. As a result, I made many decisions about myself as a woman that inhibited my sexual pleasure. Even though I hadn't yet focused on my injured sexuality, this aspect of my life healed with the LRT and rebirthing. In telling you about my present work, I'll explain how this healing came about.

I am now an LRT Trainer and I have written a book on sexuality called *Sexual Evolution*. I've led a number of seminars on sexuality over the last five years and have interviewed hundreds of people on the topic. Throughout this period, I've observed first-hand the impact that our conception, birth, and early childhood (through the fifth year) have on our sex lives. In fact, it is during these years that we receive our most significant sexual conditioning. We make major decisions about ourselves as sexual beings, and carry the effects of these decisions with us into our adult sexual lives and experiences.

My research draws a link between an individual's conception *in utero* and birth experiences, and the nature of that person's sexual habits, pleasure, and relationships. I show that the circumstances surrounding our own conception—for example, whether the pregnancy was wanted and planned, the result of a one night stand, or the product of a drunken affair—affects the way we start our *sexual* relationships. Strange as it may sound, we may be recreating our own conception every time we start a new sexual relationship.

My research also links sexual foreplay to the time you spent in the womb. For most people, the in-utero period was a loving nurturing experience, an exploration of our relationship with our mother. Similarly, foreplay is an exploration of our partner, the "getting-to-know" period of our personal relationships.

I've also observed how our birth experience itself actually affects the way we have intercourse. People who had drugs at their birth may feel the need for drugs or alcohol while making love, or they may go unconscious, or leave their body during sex. If birth was induced, or if forceps were used during delivery, a person may enjoy being seduced or induced to have sex by his or her partner. People in this category like a romantic setting to put them in the mood—candles, a foot rub, or a massage to seduce them. Quick birth individuals often prefer to have quick sex. The unique sexual style of each one of us relates to the type of birth we experienced.

What about overall patterns in our sex life? These are often based on what we learned from our parents about sex in our early childhood. What messages did you receive about your body and your sexuality? Were you given privacy and permission to explore your own sexuality as a young child? Were you taught that sex and sexual feelings were not OK, or downright bad?

Surprisingly, we often unconsciously imitate the sex life we imagined our parents had. Despite our own independent sexual experience, which should lead us to a more realistic conclusion, many of us still believe that our parents never had sex except to conceive children. If affection and sexuality were kept behind closed doors while we were growing up, we might find ourselves refraining from having sex with our partner when we would actually like to make love. It's often illuminating to realize that our parents probably had sex much more often than we imagine. They simply did a good job of hiding it. If you are using your parents as role models and are shying away from having sex with your partner to honor them, give yourself permission to go beyond what you believed to be your parent's limited sex lives.

If you grew up in an atmosphere where disapproval of sex was the norm, you may be recreating it by disapproving of yourself for being a sexual being and desiring sexual bliss. You may not be allowing yourself to have and enjoy sexual pleasure. Start approving of yourself as a sexual man or woman who deserves sexual bliss.

Birth memories are real; they affect us in later life. For instance, if you felt guilty at your birth because you believed that you hurt your mother, you may be suppressing your sexual vitality to protect your partner from being hurt by your aliveness. Unless you resolve this sense of guilt, both of you will end up short-changed. You are innocent and so is your sexuality; let go and relax.

Sometimes we are reluctant for other reasons—the intense physical emotional and psychic sensations we must confront when we have sex. Perhaps we are afraid to let go sexually because we associate orgasm with death. This association occurs in many different societies, it is not unique to our own. In France, for example, orgasm is also known as "la petite mort," or "the little death." We see this fear manifested in other parts of our sexuality as well. For instance, some men believe their semen will run out if they ejaculate too often. But this is a myth; we know that semen is their vitality, their life force. The belief that life will "run out," that there is not enough sperm, life force, or sexuality in the universe is a deathist conclusion.

A spiritual oneness is often achieved through the sexual encounter. If we embrace the philosophy of physical immortality instead of the idea that mortality is certain, sexuality becomes blissful, spiritual, and eternal. When we release our birth trauma, parental patterns, and death urge, we allow for a merging of ourselves with another in sexual spiritual bliss.

The Loving Relationships Training weekend is about change, letting go of control, and experiencing our divinity. It is about acknowledging and reclaiming our inner childlike innocence, our aliveness and immortality. After doing the LRT weekend and experiencing rebirthing, sex gets better because we recognize and release many of the patterns that keep us stuck sexually. As you go through this process of lightening up, you naturally become a vibrant, sexual being.

Overwhelm

When old patterns surface, you may feel out of control, incapacitated by confusion, as if you've had too much thrown at you at once. At LRT, we call this being in "overwhelm." It's a state you can easily fall into, particularly if you are new to processing and clearing. What some people do to cope with it, especially if they do not have a rebirther or consultant, is to withdraw or eat. Especially in couples, people often start gaining weight in an attempt to stuff the patterns back down so we can feel more "comfortable." The trouble with this solution is that then you have this new problem—being overweight—which is no fun at all. Overeating "eats away" at our confidence and self esteem, making our relationship even worse. Other unhealthy ways people deal with overwhelm are smoking, drinking, gambling, or having affairs.

I am not trying to paint a grim picture of relationships. I am only trying to warn people of what can happen when they don't stay conscious! Sometimes your patterns can get so intertwined with your partner's that you can no longer tell who is who.

When overwhelm occurs, you definitely need to breathe it out. Call your rebirther. You may even need to take a break from each other. Taking time for yourself does not mean you've failed or that you are ending the relationship. It just means you are going to go and get recentered in yourself.

In the same way, if your mate needs to take time alone, you shouldn't take that personally either. Think about it this way: in your relationship the two of you are "one" spiritually. Therefore, if your partner needs to take a break, you probably need a break, too. Look at it as an opportunity, not a threat. In fact, it would be a good idea to plan breaks from each other on a regular basis as a preventative measure instead of waiting until tensions overwhelm you both. A healthy relationship is one in which the couple can go in and out freely without attachment or clinging. If partners cannot stand to be apart, they may be inordinately attached. Many partners maintain separate interests as a way of protecting their individual selves within the relationship. This solution is healthy as long as it is a way of having your own center, not an escape from intimacy.

Know yourself well enough to recognize when you are in overwhelm, otherwise, tension can take a toll on your body and your relationship. Each partner should have his or her own private space if possible. If your house is too small for that, consider other alternatives. Where can you go to meditate? Should you move to a more spacious home? Any ideas that occur to you ought to be explored.

Mind Tracks

In the course of the years I've spent counseling people on relationships, I've had ample opportunity to watch how my clients attempt to resolve important problems in their lives. Some of their decisions may give us important insight into which ways of thinking are effective, and which ones leave us spinning our wheels.

It's surprising to find out that many people see only two mind tracks, or solutions to the important dilemas in their lives—and both of these options lead nowhere. For instance, a married woman who has felt stifled in her marriage for years may think along these lines:

> *If I stay in this relationship I will never be able to be myself and do what I want to do, but if I leave this relationship, I will not find anyone else and will be alone forever.*

A single man deliberating on whether to make a commitment to problematic partnership may limit himself this way:

> *If I get committed to this relationship, then she might leave me and the pain of abandonment would be too much to bear, but if she does not leave me, then I would have to stay in the relationship and put up with all her bullshit.*

Or the case of a dissatisfied employee, which highlights a common professional quandry:

> *If I stay in this career, then I will never get to do what I really want but if I leave this career I will not have money.*

Many clients come to see me believing that these diametrically opposed alternatives are actually the *only* options they have. Their grave error lies in using the past as a reference point. Just because relationships have gone one way in the past *does not mean* that they have to be that way in the future. For example, just because a person had two divorces *does not* mean that the third marriage will not work. Likewise, just because a person has committed to unsatisfying relationships in the past *does not* mean all future commitments will be unsatisfying. Watch out for the tendency to get yourself stuck on tracks that go nowhere, or to reinforce those tracks, adding to their effect.

During a session, when I help my clients create an alternative reality, I often suggest that they imagine the existence of a *new* railway system. The old tracks veer off to the sides, and the trains that travel along them carry the obsolete thought patterns. These trains and tracks have been officially condemned because they no longer safely serve the passenger. They are antiquated and potentially dangerous to health. What we need are brand new cars on a new track carrying fresh ideas.

An example of a "new track" would be something like this:

> *I can stay in a relationship and be myself, or I can leave and find others that are even better.*

At first the new track will feel strange or unfamiliar because the engineer is accustomed to the old track—the old thought pattern. That is exactly why it helps to picture a new track and to begin participating and strengthening in the new reality. You have to convince yourself that you can build this new reality by visualizing it, affirming it, and making it real. Before doing this you must realize that you are addicted to the old thought patterns. Begin to see the old tracks as boring, notice that they are actually repellent. Feel the excitement of the new track—and then add the final ingredient—faith. Faith is extremely important.

Even when you find yourself moving down the same old tracks, do not get discouraged. Realize that it is just a habit. Think what it is like to be an American in England, where the driver's seat is on the opposite side of the car. At first, you keep making the mistake of entering the car on the wrong side. This is a habit deeply ingrained at the age of 16. Then one day, after weeks of making the same mistake, you remember to get in on the left side. You've corrected the behavior that doesn't serve you. You have broken the habit.

Through counseling I have had the opportunity to know a number of people, both as single individuals and then afterwards as part of a couple. It has been interesting to compare how different people fared in these two situations. Some became stronger, healthier, and *more* powerful as part of a couple. Many, however, became weaker: these people actually lost self esteem, and the partners eventually caved in on themselves.

Determining why one couple grows while another couple self-destructs can be a very complicated undertaking. Indeed, so many factors contribute to the relationship's strength or weakness that it may not be possible to say exactly which ones cause a particular outcome. Certain harmful tendencies are fairly easy to identify, however, if one is trained to observe behavior in relationships. When you end up weaker instead of stronger as a result of being in a relationship, some of these types of destructive behavior are usually in evidence:

- Making the relationship top priority over everything else—neglecting the other parts of life.

- Making your mate more important than God, yourself, and everyone else. Idolizing or worshipping this person to the detriment of your own self-esteem.

- Assigning the relationship over to a priority other than spirituality.

- Attempting to become *just like* your mate and losing your individuality in the process.

- Being afraid to communicate your own ideas.

- Being afraid to confront your mate on weak areas and "stuffing" resentment about those areas.

- Protecting one's mate from productive criticism or feedback from others.

- Becoming insular, not having enough exposure to new friends and creative outlets. Getting into ruts.

- Giving your personal power away to the mate.

- The tendency for each partner to assume a set "role."

- Sinking into old family patterns.

- Lacking self-esteem.

As these habits erode each partner's self-esteem more and more, the tendencies themselves get stronger and stronger, and the couple gets *stuck*. This dynamic makes it difficult to call a halt to the destruction. Radical measures aimed at recapturing each individual's health and self-respect may be in order.

How will you know if you have found a solid, positive relationship? It won't be hard to tell. A negative, unholy relationship feels depleting, like a depressing burden. But a healthy, holy relationship is a whole different game. It nourishes each mate's individuality, strength, power, creativity, and productivity in the world. Each partner has no personal spiritual life and considers their spirituality the top priority—the relationship comes second. There is a spontaneity and moment-by-moment flow between real human beings rather than rigid role playing by two-dimensional caricatures. Each partner feels safe to give the other constructive feedback that produces *movement*—within the relationship there is no fear of communicating *anything*. Each person easily maintains a high degree of self-esteem because both partners are constantly centered in spirituality. Each partner supports the other's "coming out" and getting into power, and is not threatened or jealous of these efforts. Each knows how to process family patterns that come up without getting stuck. The techniques the two have created for clearing problems work because everything they do is *life supporting*, and synergy and harmony abound.

Addictions

Let's talk more about obstacles that prevent us from having a healthy partnership. Are you in an addictive relationship? Do you consistently lay aside your own needs for the sake of your relationship? Do you feel as though the relationship has you in its grip, has taken over your life, and you have given yourself over to it? Do you suffer endlessly on account of the relationship? Do you lose your boundaries in the relationship? Are you addicted *to* relationships? Do you "attach" to the other in a very dependent way? Do you use the other person to escape the life you have constructed for yourself? Do you define everything in your existence in terms of your relationship? Do you "hang in there" way past the point of sanity? Do you shut off your feelings and awareness in service to the relationship?

If you answered yes to any of the questions above, you need to take a serious look at your relationship addictions!

Anne Wilson Schaef's book, *Escape from Intimacy*, gives us a clear picture of how to tell the difference between an addictive and a healthy relationship. I recommend that you read it along with her other books, including *When Society Becomes an Addict*, in which the author thoroughly covers the topic of sexual and relationship addictions. Schaef explains that there are two main categories of relationship addiction. In the first, the individual is addicted to having a relationship—any relationship, real or fantasized. In the second, the person is addicted to a particular person. In the first type, the addiction centers around an *idea*, while the second type centers around a *person*. The latter, Schaef aptly points out, is more like having a *hostage* than a *relationship*.

While it is valuable to read Schaef's book for its description of relationship addiction, it is extremely important that we face the topic of addiction in general. *A Course in Miracles* tells us that "a special relationship is the ego's chief weapon, (text, p. 317) to keep us so distracted that we "forget God." Indeed, this may be the greatest danger we face from an unholy or addictive partnership.

Being addicted to the illusion of romance is one of the most powerful traps in our society. We have been brainwashed by society and by the commercial media into believing that we should wait to fall in love with the "perfect one," the "right one," someone who will sweep us off our feet in a flood of passion, or drive us so wild that we cannot get them out of our mind! This is, among other things, a rather adolescent view of love. We may well have had such deep infatuations as teenagers and have yet to change our idea that "true love" means we must constantly feel overwhelming sensations. If we don't, we assume our love interest cannot be the "right" one.

Psychologists have tried to tell us that the experience of falling in love can be likened to temporary insanity in that we use both to escape reality. But because the media's version of love is broadcasted full-force, the addiction to the romantic illusion has been entrenched in our society.

Addicted to this illusion, you may not even notice the potential mates that could offer you *true* love. If you happen to find a mate, you may become infatuated for a while, but as the infatuation begins to wear off, there is a good chance that you may blame your new partner. Without a sense of perspective, you may break off the relationship before true love has a chance to grow; you may be tempted to have an affair, or leave, since leaving seems to provide a way to get the next "fix."

Flawless relations are illusionary: real partnerships between real people go through periods of difficulty as well as smooth sailing. That's just the way it is. Feeling ambivalent about your relationship from time to time may, therefore, be a sign that you are moving in the direction of a more healthy love! If you say to yourself, "Why should I settle for anything less than perfect?" and reject your mate the minute they expose a flaw, you could be setting up a syndrome of failure. Dr. Frank Pittman, author of *Private Lies: Infidelity and the Betrayal of Intimacy,* writes that people who behave in this way "aren't really looking for the 'perfect' person at all! They are looking for some reason to reject all imperfect people, because if they ever found the 'right one,' they would have to *share.* Resistance to sharing is the real issue." (Now *that* is something to think about!)

Our era has been dubbed the "age of noncommitment and the epoch of half-heartedness." Isn't compulsive avoidance of commitment the sign of another addiction? Both *having to be* in a relationship all the time and continually *avoiding* one can be addictive behavior.

In the same way, we can also be addicted to *longing* rather than *having.* If you are accustomed to the intense sensation of yearning for someone over a long period of time, you may end up coveting this sensation, and then *having* might not even satisfy you.

Take a close look at yourself and see if you are actually addicted to *not* getting what you want. By being accustomed to getting the short end of the stick, you can perpetuate other bad habits such as complaining, getting angry, feeling cheated, and blaming. After all, if you get what you need, you might feel less entitled to feel the dissatisfaction you are so familiar with. If you were to get everything you wanted, *what could you be angry about?*

This is not an easy process. I know. I have had to deal with many of the addictions I just mentioned. The only things that have worked for me to get through it all are prayer and spiritual purification. The changes you will experience affect your body as well as your emotions. One has to also be willing to go through a physical shift required by the body to overcome psychological addiction. Such changes *can* be made—and it is definitely worth the struggle. And it *does* get easier. After a while, all addictions become intolerable. As you learn to love yourself, you will become disciplined. You simply won't accept them anymore.

Review

1. Study your conception trauma. Observe how you conceive relationships.

2. Be aware how the incest taboo may be affecting your relationship when one partner is not as committed as the other.

3. Constantly check and see if you are in a strengthening relationship or a weakening relationship.

4. Do not hurry into a permanent mating because of sexual desire, then later rationalize destructive interactions.

5. Know what your reasons are for mating. Are you doing so out of sexual attraction, because of past-life ties, or a cosmic tie based on service?

6. Try to mate on all planes equally. Before mating seriously, contact a very reliable spiritual psychic guide and astrologer.

7. The problem-solving techniques that you use early on can be habit forming, so make sure that you set up positive, constructive ones as soon as you begin a relationship. Give and receive constructive feedback from one another.

8. Always tell the whole truth; share all your feelings and admit it when your "case" is up.

9. Early in your relationship, discuss your purposes in life and priorities.

10. Do not use the past as a reference point. Do not impose the exact same kind of relationship you had with the last person on your current mate.

11. Watch for ways that you may be avoiding intimacy. Also watch for ways that you are smothering the relationship by being together too much.

12. Remember that not only is it *okay* to take breaks from each other, it is *healthy*.

13. When you become agitated because your patterns are up or you are feeling overwhelmed, use spiritual purification techniques instead of liquor, drugs, or food.

14. Try to avoid letting your mind get stuck on two tracks that are going nowhere. Always go for solutions. Visualize new "tracks," new "trains," new horizons.

15. Stop "role playing."

16. Get out of denial about addictions. Work on clearing addictions of all types in your relationship.

17. Be on the look-out for a need for romantic "fixes" that prevent you from having a real relationship. Watch out for the tendency to find something wrong with your mate so that you have reason to get rid of the relationship instead of learning tolerance and sharing.

· PART III ·

Relationship Dynamics

The Illusion of Ego

A Course in Miracles tells us that all human conflicts stem from the fact that we do not recognize ourselves, our brothers, or even God. We make them strangers by misperceiving them. And having turned them into "the other," we attack our brothers (paraphrase, text, p. 35). Such judgment always involves rejection; the choice to judge our brother rather than to *know* him causes loss of peace (paraphrase, text, p. 42).

Let's begin, then, to know ourselves, to get clear on who we are. This beautiful passage in *A Course in Miracles* can be the starting point.

What Am I

I am God's Son, complete and healed and whole, shining in the reflection of His love. In me is His creation sanctified and guaranteed eternal life. In me is love perfected, fear impossible, and joy established without opposite. I am the holy home of God Himself. I am the Heaven where His love resides. I am His holy Sinlessness Itself, for in my purity abides His Own (workbook, p. 469).

This is your *true reality.* Nothing else is real. You were made in the image of God. You were made perfect. Perfection is your reality. You mistakenly think you can make imperfect what was made perfect. You made the mistake of thinking you were separate from God and then you made up your own separate self which is not real, because it is impossible to be separate from God. Therefore your ego, which is the separated self, is not real. Only your perfection is real.

Your brother is like you. Your sister is like you. All of humanity is like you. See in your sisters and brothers (mates) God's creation. He or she is a mirror of yourself.

1. Would it be possible for you to hate your brother if you were like him?

2. Could you attack him if you realized you journey with him toward the same goal?

3. Wouldn't you help him reach it in every way you could, if his attainment of it were perceived as yours?

Your brother is your friend because his Father created him like you. There is no difference (paraphrase, text. p. 465–466).

The Course forewarns us that we may oppose its teachings precisely because they reveal that each of us is like all others. There can never be true harmony among those who are different, for the pursuit of specialness will always bring pain (paraphrase, text, p. 466–467).

You must perceive your brother only as you see him *now.* Find the present. His past has no reality in the present. See him without his past. Perceive him as born again. His errors are all past, and by perceiving him without them, you are releasing him—and yourself.

See the Holy Spirit in your brother. See his innocence. See his perfection. The present offers your brothers in the light you can share with them—and in so doing you free your past. Would you then hold the past against them? If you do, you are choosing to remain in darkness (paraphrase, text, p. 233).

The Illusion of Inequality

Inequality is an illusion. The idea that you are unequal comes from low self-esteem, a subject I have written about at length. Feeling unequal is the flip side of believing you are "special" or different from other people. For feeling unequal also stems from forgetting who you are, forgetting the truth of your being.

When you remember that you are *God expressing*, just as every-one else is, it is impossible to feel unequal. For instance, you may feel frustrated that even though you know deep down that you and your mate are equals, you find yourself constantly focusing on all the things your mate can do and you can't! What a frustrating thought pattern to deal with! If you understood the Course's message you would realize that the differences in your skills are insignificant, because *all differences are temporary* (paraphrase, manual, p. 8). We are all part of the divine Oneness. Jesus taught us that we can even be like *Him*. He just happened to complete himself perfectly before anyone else.

In addition to low self-esteem, you may be harboring negative thoughts that originated at your own birth. These negative ideas can also make you *feel* unequal. In the Loving Relationships Training we call these thoughts our "personal lies." They include:

"I am not good enough"

"I am bad"

"I am wrong"

"I am guilty"

"I am weak"

"I am not perfect"

"There is something wrong with me"

"I am a failure"

We have discussed the negative impact of this kind of thinking in many of the publications we at LRT have written or recommended.

One of the most important points these books relay is that these "personal lies" may be unconscious. They may be conclusions you made at birth which, if left uncorrected, can permanently destroy your self-esteem. We are always "wrestling" with these until we let go of them.

In truth, the most negative thought you can possibly have about yourself is the myth "I am separate." This is the ultimate personal lie, and if you believe in it, it is the idea most destructive to your life. When we wallow in these personal invalidations without making an attempt to change them, we commit the equivalent of "taking the name of the Lord in vain." When we follow the words "I am" with a negative idea, we invalidate our divinity and misuse its power. By affirming these untruths we deny the God-Self in us!

In *A Course in Miracles*, it is written: "be not content with littleness" (text, p. 285) because you will never have peace . . . you won't think you deserve it. Over and over, we limit or broaden our horizons based on our own perceptions. Let's work toward becoming as magnificent as we can be.

Communication

The ability to communicate well often seems to be an innate talent some of us have and some of us don't, or a simple matter of timing and good techniques. These factors certainly facilitate communication, but others—especially self-knowledge and high self-esteem—play an equally important role. When you are more certain of who you are, and see yourself as an equal, communication with others improves a great deal. You are no longer afraid to express yourself, or to speak up and ask for what you want. You are neither quiet nor loud, hesitant nor pushy. You are spontaneous and your words come out just right. Good communication has become a natural expression of your divinity.

If you are having trouble communicating, you need to find out what the source of the problem is. Why do you have this communication block? What is the negative thought that causes it?

If you grew up in a household where parents gave each other the silent treatment, where one family member dominated everything with his or her communication, where people were afraid to say what they felt, or where it was not safe to tell the truth, you were taught on a model that actually *impeded* rather than promoted communication. You will have to throw off these fetters. You *can* and you *should*. There is absolutely no need to spend your whole life communicating poorly just because your family did. You may have learned their habits, but you can *unlearn* them, too.

Because I was verbally punished for saying the truth to my father as a child, I used to have a fear of telling the total truth to men I loved. I would always say just what I thought men wanted to hear. Ultimately, I ended up going into therapy over this. Through practice, I overcame my block against telling the truth, and now I *always* say what I feel—and people, including men, always know how I feel. No one feels duped, and I feel strong and whole. They like it and I like it. It feels good. The truth works.

We have a motto in the Loving Relationships Training which is "Tell the complete truth faster and there is more fun per hour." In other words, the sooner you tell the truth, the more you will enjoy life. Here is a simple exercise in telling the truth: You let your mate tell you all their feelings on a subject for 15 minutes straight. You listen without interrupting. Then you tell them back what you thought they said. Now switch roles and begin the exercise again. This feedback technique will help you see how well you are listening and communicating.

Here is another learning exercise: You tell your mate, "Something I saw as a child but felt I could not communicate was ＿＿," or, "Something I feel I can't communicate now is ＿＿," filling in the blanks. If too much fear comes up, say, "The reasons I'm afraid to communicate this are ＿＿," completing the sentence with clear-sighted and honest reflections. Notice how you feel about yourself and your partner before and afterwards.

What do you notice about the two processes above? What tone do these particular questions set? If you use these techniques, you'll soon recognize what a difference politeness, respect, and clear boundaries make! An open mind, willing to accept and acknowledge your partner's efforts and ability to change, actually facilitate those shifts in behavior! Telling the truth faster does not imply the sacrifice of graciousness. Relentless nagging can only spoil steps forward. There are much more effective means than nagging.

Stop and ask yourself why you are saying something in a way that the other person can't hear. The way to be heard is to say what you have to say without blame. Once someone perceives blame in what you're saying, their options are to blame back, or tune you out. For instance, if you accuse your partner of never helping with the dishes, the implication is that they are a bad person, they've failed in some way. Instead, if you explain that you're tired by the end of the week and need help around the house, you'd be much more likely to get it. If your partner is doing the nagging, choose to hear it not as blame, but simply as information. For instance, if they accuse you of not picking up your clothes, you can thank them for reminding you. If you find yourself actually picking a fight, this may be a cover for a deeper problem. If your partner wants to have sex and you don't, they may not say anything at the time. However, in the morning, they may find fault with something as trivial as the way you prepared breakfast. If a fight ensues, rest assured it has very little to do with breakfast and much more to do with releasing tension and anger, consequently circumventing the real issue: rejection. Nagging will not reveal the true issue at hand. Patience and understanding will.

Conforming and Rebelling

Day in and day out, do you tend to rebel or conform—or have you transcended those tendencies and become your own self? How about your mate—is she or he a conformist or a rebel? This is good information to have. During childhood, we generally conform to our parent's wishes or rebel against them. We may be doing some of both, but usually one pattern is stronger. While these behavior patterns are normal in childhood and adolescence, they do not serve us so well in our adult lives. We must either face and resolve this childhood-based tendency, or risk causing perpetual conflict in our adult relationships.

If you have set your mate up as one of your parents, you then may end up doing nearly everything they say (conforming) or doing everything in opposition to their wishes (rebelling). Either way, your behavior is reactive. You are not responding in the *present*. You are still in the past. Your mate might suggest something to you; if you tend to conform, you may do as they ask even if you don't really like the idea and even if it is not actually good for you. And later, there is a good chance you will resent it. If you are the rebel, on the other hand, your mate might suggest something perfectly reasonable, but you may very likely refuse even though it might be a lot of fun. Again, you both get ripped off.

Go back in your mind and review your childhood history. What was your role in the family? If family members were to label you either a conformer or a rebel, which term would they use?

Now consider your past relations. Did your "knee-jerk" rebelliousness cause conflict where none existed? Did it make a relatively fair partner seem like someone you had to fight against? Or was your tendency to conform, letting yourself be manipulated until your partner lost respect for you—or until you lost your sense of self? More importantly, take a good look at your current relationship. What forces are at play now? Have you processed your childhood tendencies to conform or rebel? These are your issues—sometimes you will have to process them away from your mate. If these old tendencies are still influencing your behavior, take responsibility for them, and begin the work to change them.

Sibling Rivalry

In the last few years we at LRT have been studying patterns related to sibling rivalry. But in the early years of the training, we overlooked this subject so completely that it was not even touched upon in our work. Why had we so totally "tuned out" these issues? When we first discovered the lapse, we couldn't make any sense of it. But, with time, we saw that the reasons were not so mysterious after all. In fact, our "oversight" was characteristic of one of the most common reactions children have to new siblings: they "tune them out." This was no coincidence. As I dug deeper, I began to see all kinds of competition showing up in the organization the last few years. Naturally, we had to go back and handle this topic in our own "home."

You may believe—as we at first did—that you don't have friction in your life stemming from sibling rivalry. But look more closely. Jealousy or rivalry often begins before the new baby is born. Children reason, "Why would mother want a new baby unless the old one [me] was not good enough?" Confirming this occurence, the Obstetrics Department of the University of Minnesota has issued a very interesting pamphlet on the subject of sibling rivalry. It points out that young children express their feelings and uncertainties about the coming of a new baby through a variety of behavior patterns.

> [Quite often older siblings wet their] pants or bed, ask for a bottle, want to breastfeed, act silly, ask for more attention, be whiny, talk baby talk, cry a lot, cling to you, be demanding, stutter, have temper tantrums, suggest "it" be sent back to the hospital or put in the garbage, inquire whether babies ever die, hug baby boa-constrictor style, rock baby too rapidly, hit, bite, scream, spit, punch, push, have nightmares, dream of pushing baby out of window, have wheezing, coughing, or vomiting attacks, consistently tease or tattle, become sarcastic, have continual accidents, exaggerated fears, or skin rashes, bite nails, pluck hair, seek popularity through constant competitiveness or become a wallflower and avoid competition.

This avalanche of responses is really quite amazing isn't it? If small children have such intense physical and emotional reactions to their sibling's existence, surely the effects on our adult life are also profound.

One of the reactions to this experience which often stays with us into our adulthood is the belief that love was limited. If, as a child, we think that we had to compete for our parent's love, we become addicted to a "win-lose" mentality. In the LRT, we now do processes that help people recall sibling rivalry, winning, losing, and decisions about competition. We find out who they did *not* want to win—both in the past and the present. Then we ask the group members to close their eyes and imagine both adversaries winning. Astonishingly enough, people *cannot imagine it*. Our mind is so addicted to thinking "if I win, someone else has to lose," that it cannot conceive of any other outcome.

I'm certain you can imagine how this attitude can ruin a loving relationship. Its detrimental effect begins as soon as competition sets in. It can be very overt or very covert. This attitude may surface over all kinds of issues: money, sex, power struggles, or raising kids. I once counseled a couple who even competed over enlightenment! She was mad at him because he would not get rebirthed and do seminars. And he was just as reactive. He would not go along with her requests precisely because she wanted him to; for him, this would have meant that she had "won" and he had "lost" by doing what she wanted! And so their dance of frustration and resentment repeated its cycle over and over again.

Competition in sports and the workplace may produce excellent athletes or employees, but competition in personal relationships can be deadly. You may not be conscious that you are competing with your mate; it all can be very subtle. According to traditional ways of solving problems in relationships, you and your partner place the problem between you and battle it out for who is "right." This arrangement is about antagonism. A relationship, however, is not a tennis match. It may be a game, but it should be a game where both win, where both you and your mate are on the *same* side, looking at the problem in front of you—not between you. You are team members striving for the highest good. Though it may sound utopian, developing this perspective is actually possible. But it requires cooperation, enlightenment, and good techniques to resolve conflict.

The Cold War was a striking example of the ultimate horror that sibling rivalry could produce. That terrifying standoff has cost us ten trillion dollars—money that surely could have been put to better use. We must learn to work together on the personal level, adopting a win-win mentality so that we may reap the immense benefits of global unity. For cooperation results in synergy, letting you become creative and ecstatically alive.

Double Messages: The Yes-No Problem

I rarely walk out of a movie; I don't usually attend movies I wouldn't like. But when I do find myself in a movie theater watching a film I can't stand, it usually means that there is a lesson there that I must pay attention to.

This is what happened once when I was taking a rest in Toronto for several days before a workshop I was scheduled to give there. Making plans for the evening, I thought going to a movie would be relaxing. The women I was staying with agreed. We picked a foreign film that was supposed to be a sexy comedy and very good. Arriving at the theater, we bought our tickets, snacks, and drinks and found our places. Settling into the comfortable seats, we laughed and joked until the lights dimmed, looking forward to the show. But we were in for a surprise.

The film turned out to be one of the most wrenching and upsetting I have ever seen. My friends and I all wanted to leave, but kept staying on longer, thinking that the plot would take a turn for the better. We were mistaken. Three-quarters of the way through, when we finally got up and walked out, several other members of the audience left as well.

The film was especially jarring to my hosts and me because we had just spent four glorious days meditating, praying, chanting, and practicing devotions together. We had been getting really high. But the film brought us face to face with an aspect of life we did not want to deal with. It revolved around unresolved sexual obsessions, and didn't strike me as one bit funny. It was agony. Throughout the entire story, the energy of the film was *yes-no*: "I want you and I will tease you, but I will never give in to you." Anyone who is the least bit sensitive to energy would go away feeling that they had been need-lessly toyed with or "jerked around."

Though watching the film left us with a deep sense of dissatisfac-tion, I am sure its directors felt they were representing true life. For many people, they probably were. And so, in the end, the film's dissatisfying theme made me *think*. When we arrived at the house, my companions and I decided to look at all the ways we gave double messages to people in our lives. The tally ended up much greater than we'd imagined. Each in her own way clearly needed to see that film, and each of us were humbled accordingly.

Just what are double messages? They happen all the time. A person may say "I really want you to be with me," while conveying "don't get close to me" in the same breath.

"I really love you but I really hate you."

"I really want a relationship that works but nothing you do is right."

"I really want to succeed but don't make me come out of the womb."

"I really want you to make a lot of money but I wish you would stop working so hard and abandoning me."

By paying close attention, we can often discover a whole range of examples in our own lives. We claim to want one thing, but our behavior creates just the opposite outcome. These "mixed" messages confuse others and cause us to become angry because we aren't getting what we want in our relationships. This continuous cycle of double messages and frustration will leave your body a wreck.

If giving double messages describe the modus operandi of you or your partner, you may also end up feeling discouraged about being able to clear anything in your relationship. It *is* hard to clear up *any* kind of relationship when one or both members do not see that they are sending double messages to others, and sometimes even to themselves. Let me illustrate what I mean. A person who conveys the message "I want to have sex with you," and then does not allow love-making to follow has traditionally been labeled a "tease" and we generally look upon such a person with distain. But simple condemnation prevents us from asking the deeper questions. Let's look at why someone might act that way. Perhaps they want to get even with the opposite sex. Or maybe they are too scared to come into intimate contact with a real person or don't think they deserve pleasure—or perhaps their feigned seductiveness stems from a combination of these factors.

Although we may most often associate double messages with sexual interactions, they actually come up all the time in all different areas of life as well. Whether it's around sex, children, commitment, or power relations, yes-no energy *always* reveals unresolved conflict and a lack of self-knowledge. To avoid this set-up, you not only have to know what you want, you have to communicate it clearly, making sure your message is free of counterintentions.

Let's say your partner tells you they want peace—but subconsciously they believe, "I need anger in order to survive," or, "anger makes me feel powerful." It would be hard to find a technique that would effectively bring them tranquility because their underlying thoughts would sabotage peace. As long as their subconscious beliefs go unchallenged, they will have the tendency to unconsciously set up conflicts and manipulate events to go badly so that they would have an excuse to get angry. This person does not really want peace, they would rather be angry. They may insist, "But I do want peace. I just can't contain my anger." Pointing to their lack of control as an excuse and her anger as a sort of addiction is no answer. Their only addiction, in this case, is their refusal to get off it.

One of the most difficult jobs we have in life is to look deeply within ourselves, acknowledging, along with our nobler feelings, our errors, pettiness, and lack of love. It isn't easy to admit we may be giving others double messages. But if you are frustrating and hurting people around you in this way, take responsibility for it. Ambivalence that stems from laziness creates a *no-win* situation. And if you are the one being jerked around by someone else in this way, you must take responsibility for it also. Why do you need to be treated in this way? Why should you participate in a no-win situation?

When we are clear, our actions match our words. We neither convey mixed messages, nor harbor "hidden agendas." It becomes easy for others to give us what we ask for because the request has been openly communicated. When we feel these good feelings, we can be sure we have conquered the rule of the ego. Clarity in the mind of the Holy Spirit is just that: clear, easy, smooth, rewarding, satisfying energy.

Staying in the Now

I've mentioned the importance of being present. Staying in the now is blissful magic if you truly love life. And you *will* love life more if you do stay present: it's a miraculous cycle. Staying in the now means that you are not projecting the past onto the present. It means you are not worrying about the future. You are one hundred percent alive and loving *now*. There is nothing else than the passion of *this* moment, which you want to experience totally, offering your excellence.

Why does this way of being seem so hard to capture? It is only because we foul up the magic of the present with our egos. In the beginning of *A Course in Miracles* there is a lesson that reads, "I see only the past" (workbook, p. 11). That lesson forces us to look at our addiction to projecting the past onto the present. The fact is, we are not just here in the present looking at our mate as he is now. We are usually seeing him as our father, or her as our mother, sibling, obstetrician, or someone else. We are not looking clearly at reality. We are loading up our past fears and doubts onto the energy of life, leaving it no chance to flow freely.

The Course also tells us that we are "never upset for the reason we think" (workbook, p. 8). Instead, an earlier, similar event is upsetting us and we are blaming the wrong sources for our angry or painful feelings. The fundamental cause of bad feelings is always the ego, the illusion of separation—not the superficially apparent problem.

If we can stay in the moment without projecting the past onto the present moment, or worrying about the future, and if we can let the fullness of life rush in, living forever will become easy. Our relationships will be filled with vitality, and the spontaneity will make us as happy as children.

In a sense, being in the present is *being out of control*—and human beings generally fear being out of control. We believe something terrible will result. But, in fact, the opposite is true. When we are in *control,* our ego obstructs life's natural flow—and there the trouble begins. Being out of *control* means you are allowing the Holy Spirit to roll through you without any hindrances. It's exciting. It's fun. It's creative. And it is *not* scary. Being out of control means giving up fear (for fear *is* control). Being out of control returns us to our natural state. Staying totally in the present is the key to enlightenment and vitality!

Review

1. Get clear on who you and your mate are spiritually.

2. See any other person—your mate, your relative, acquaintance, or stranger—as yourself. How can you hate or attack them if they are you? Since they are you, you should help them reach their goals.

3. When looking at another, always stay in the present. Let the past go. See them in the present, without condemnation.

4. See the Holy Spirit in your mate and in everyone. See their perfection.

5. Do not make the other person's ego (or "case") real, or you will be reinforcing it in yourself.

6. Remember that the first obstacle to peace is the desire to get rid of peace.

7. When your relationship is stuck, work on your *own* case instead of blaming your mate.

8. When you are supporting someone and they cannot accept it, realize that they may have you set up as their obstetrician or vice versa.

9. When someone is supporting you and you don't think it feels like support, perhaps you have them set up as your obstetrician. You can say, "This feels like an attack. Maybe I am projecting onto you."

10. Never perceive yourself as unjustly treated. Remember you are creating every reaction you get from someone. Consider that this reaction may be a result of your karma.

11. Do not give your power away. Know that your opinions count. The other person's opinions count as well. Space must be created for both opinions.

12. Know whether you are into "victim consciousness" or your God-power. You must know the difference.

13. If you stay connected to love and the Source, you will be able to think from your center and for yourself.

14. Don't try to change the world. Change the way you view the world.

15. Handle your personal lies (personal subconscious invalidations).

16. Remember, only in our magnificence will we be satisfied.

17. Recognize the communication pattern in your blood family. Was it positive or negative? Figure out if you are copying it. Should you continue it?

18. The truth works. Tell the complete truth as quickly as you can.

19. Practice the feedback exercises in this chapter to make sure your communication is heard correctly.

20. Know yourself. Are you a conformist or a rebel? How does this make you respond to your mate's suggestions?

21. Be aware if you are competing with anyone. Who is it that you do not want to win? Always have a cooperation mentality, not a win-lose mentality.

22. Mean what you say at all times. Do not give double messages or withhold information. Your actions should match your words. Know what you want and how to communicate it without counter intentions.

23. Know that the key to vitality is to stay in the present. Give up your fear of being out of control.

PART IV

Relationship Clearing

Getting Yourself Unstuck

In working toward righting a relationship, you must first learn how to get yourself "unstuck." The first step—realizing that you have reached an impass—sounds deceptively easy. The truth is that many of us are in denial about this basic problem. Because of how much resistance we have against admitting we have problems at all, I've listed seven signs that will help you recognize when you are stuck:

- You feel unhappy and isolated.
- You feel anxious or moody, rarely experiencing joy.
- You feel helpless, can't move forward or accomplish ordinary projects and activities.
- You are sick, in pain, as if your vital energy is blocked.
- You feel a nagging urge to attack someone verbally or physically.
- You can't get your personal relationship to clear.
- Your financial situation is shaky or faltering.

If you've experienced any of these difficulties, you'll need to give yourself some special attention. The situation calls for a spiritual purification. In my book, *Pure Joy,* I list over twenty different techniques. Rebirthing, chanting, reading *A Course in Miracles,* and prayer are the ones I use most frequently. If you are unable to do any of these techniques, you can write down your negative thoughts on a piece of paper and change them into affirmations. This will at least give you some immediate relief.

Another writing technique I use for clearing is to compose a letter to God and place it on my altar. In the message I bare my soul, but I do not plead to God to take my problems away. Instead, you should *confess* your case, describing your negative thoughts and addictions to those thoughts. Offer your words up to the Holy Spirit, Jesus, Babaji, or whatever works for you. Decide that you will think differently, and ask God to strengthen your new thoughts with energy. This technique always works for me. I have written my Master, Babaji, in this way for years and afterwards, usually I release my anxiety by crying. Then, if I've been stuck, I can let go and trust again.

Of course, preventing problems is the best policy to pursue. Spiritual purification keeps us from getting stuck. But during times when we feel at a complete impasse, so stuck that we don't even feel like breathing, when we may not feel like praying, writing, or chanting—this is what I recommend: get your tape-recorder and earphones, put on some chanting tapes with mantras such as *Om Namaha Shivai,* and turn the volume way up. Lie down in front of your altar and relax until you break through the impasse. Take some deep breaths and let yourself cry. It *works.*

Assisting in the Clearing Process

Until we are all spiritual masters and constantly holy, we will have things to clear. Thus, in any relationship, difficulties or conflicts will come up that need to be processed. The way in which we do this can make or break a positive relationship.

The old, unenlightened way of dealing with conflicts was to find things wrong with the other person, to pick on them, to point out faults continually; in other words, to make the other person wrong. As you may well know, this road leads nowhere.

If both you and your partner are on the path of enlightenment, however, and equally involved in spiritual purification to clear yourselves, processing can even be enjoyable. You can make helping each other clear into a game. At the same time you must avoid the mistake of "over-processing" your mate. Otherwise, your relationship may come to resemble a continuous therapy session, which is not the proper purpose of your union.

When the clearing process involves two partners, it should be based on certain agreements—a sort of "protocol." The partner who needs clearing can ask for the support of their mate, or the person who is more clear at the time can offer their help. Never process someone without their permission—a person has to *want* to get off it on their own. Even if you believe you have the answer to your partner's problems, your truth will have no effect if they are not open to hearing it. As a partner, your job is to let them clear themselves in your presence by being there for them, and by offering them a higher thought when they are ready. They may happen upon the higher thought by themselves. You can listen and ask questions until they discover it.

During a session, if my client is stuck in a great deal of pain and misery and wants assistance, I begin by finding out if they are willing to look for the thought that is causing their misery. I am careful of my tone, so that they do not feel I am making them wrong for having a negative thought. I want them to know I am not trying to change them—the person who they really are. I am merely available to help them let go of destructive thoughts *if* and only *if* they feel ready. After establishing that my client is willing to search deeply, I might serve them by asking, "What negative thought is causing this pain?" Such a question often helps locate the deeply buried thought. In answering my question and verbalizing their thoughts, my client begins to release their emotions.

Once in a while a client simply refuses to look at their thoughts. I gently try to assist them in understanding why. If it is appropriate, I help them to see that they might feel better if they examined their thoughts. If they can't hear my advice, I don't force the point. Most people come back for help when they are ready.

If you consistently find that your mate does not want to look at any of their thoughts, you will have to suggest they find their own methods for clearing. If they refuse to clear themselves *at all*, then the relationship could prove very difficult in the long run. For a relationship to succeed, both parties really have to be willing to confront problems. If your mate is not at all willing, then you must ask yourself the following questions:

- What is my payoff for being with someone who is not willing to clear?

- How does this situation mirror my past?

- Am I using this person to hold me back?

- Before I give up, have I considered the fact that he may be truly terrified? Does he perhaps need support in the area of fear?

To prevent the habit of "over-processing" each other, it is a good idea for each of you to have your own private rebirther. In an ideal arrangement you would get rebirthed once every week or two by a trained rebirther, then come back and share your experience in a light way with your mate. You might ask your partner to support you in further releasing those blocks by seeing you as healed.

At the Loving Relationships Training, we advise against mates rebirthing each other. As I've mentioned before, it is essential that you prevent your relationship from becoming a continuous therapy session and avoid the danger of setting each other up as the obstetrician. Just the same, it is valuable to be able to handle a rebirthing, in case your mate goes into a spontaneous rebirthing late at night and you do not feel it is appropriate to get your rebirther out of bed! If you read the books we at LRT have written on this subject, such as *Ideal Birth* and *Rebirthing in the New Age*, you will feel knowledgeable enough to be of assistance in an emergency. If you have been rebirthed yourself, you may intuitively know what to do; perhaps you can remember how your rebirther served you. But why not take a course in rebirthing others?

Supporting someone who wants to clear themselves can be magic when the following ingredients are present:

- Your friend expressly asks for support from you.

- You give them total attention in an environment that is nurturing. You are not distracted.

- You have an attitude of love and acceptance and compassion. You listen. You are careful not to make judgments or put out negative energy.

- You have permission to ask them questions, and you word them in such a way as to help them locate their own answers.

- You hold the belief that they are perfect and healed and can overcome this.

- You get permission to offer them a higher thought if appropriate, but first create the space so that they may discover it themselves.

- You thank them for the opportunity to serve, and continue to hold the highest thoughts possible for them in their absence after you part.

This process can be relatively problem-free if you are helping someone with troubles that don't involve you. If you yourself are personally involved, you can still go ahead and use the same process. But you must be willing to have her do the same clearing on you. In other words, you must also be willing to honestly look at *your own part* in the problem. If the atmosphere is too charged with tension, however, and you are unable to work together in a supportive way, you should agree to get a third party who is skilled at assisting in clearing, and who is not emotionally involved in the problem.

Never hesitate to lay your relationship at the feet of a qualified person who is more enlightened or more clear than you are at the time. Do not be embarrassed; your willingness can save you years of hassle! I know couples who won't tell anyone they're having problems because they want to "look good." These couples rip themselves off. I've met other couples who never mention their problems because they believe that one should never "air dirty laundry." They inherited the conviction from their parents that it is bad to expose anything. Quite frankly, there are times when we cannot solve our problems by ourselves. We need support, and we need someone who is not emotionally involved in the dilemma. An enlightened friend can be a relationship saver. Not only may they offer an unexpected solution, they may guide us to the right rebirther or the right books.

By the time a person finally gets to a rebirther they have often read our books or taken the Loving Relationships Training. They usually know the value of rebirthing and feel safe doing it in groups. I learned a long time ago that "what you try to hide in the closets will be shouted from the rooftops." You might as well take hold of the process and embrace it.

Everyone has problems—don't get upset by yours, just go for solutions. The dynamic you use for problem-solving and achieving solutions should be enjoyable and invigorating, "a win" for you *and* your partner. You should get *high* doing it. If you are exhausted by the process, or feel competitive or resentful about it, you are off track.

When you notice that your old methods aren't working, it's time to figure out a new method that makes life smoother. A good general rule when resolving conflict is *to deal with only one issue at a time.* Resolve the problem under discussion before bringing up other ones.

When two people are having a major dispute they cannot resolve themselves, they may agree to seek the assistance of a mediator. Once, a mediation expert from New Zealand, reminded me of a simple but very effective conflict resolution technique that works well in this context. Naturally, it is best to seek someone fairly well trained in mediating personal conflicts.

The mediator begins by asking one person to give their version of the problem. The other partner listens with complete attention and without interruption, making every effort to see the point of view of the first speaker. As you can imagine, it is harder for a couple to do this alone, since one person may be tempted to interrupt, fight back, or defend. The mediator's presence prevents retorts and interruptions. After the first speaker completes their account, the person who was listening tells their version. This simple step clears the air and takes the pressure off because each party finally feels *heard.* The mediator can then help the couple strive for the highest spiritual thoughts on the subject and complete the process.

Here are some helpful meditations on this subject from *A Course in Miracles*.

- Truth cannot deal with errors that you want

- It is not up to you to change your brother, but merely to accept him as he is. Any attempt you make to correct a brother means that you believe correction by you is possible and this can only be the arrogance of the ego

- When a situation has been dedicated wholly to truth, peace is inevitable

Settling Arguments

Most arguments start when two people have different opinions and each one asserts that his is right and the other's is wrong. Here's a method to break this pattern. It is called the Highest Spiritual Thought Game. Both people involved in a conflict must agree to play the game whenever this polarization occurs. Both must begin by abandoning their positions, starting with a clean slate. And both partners must agree to search for the highest spiritual thought that could resolve the issue. In other words, the highest spiritual thought is the most loving, the most positive, and it feels the best in your body. When such a thought presents itself, everone involved will have a feeling of joy and relief; it doesn't matter who thought of the idea first. It could be either partner—or the maid, the secretary, or a child.

If my mate happens to channel the highest spiritual thought, I agree to get off my lower position and go up to his. I don't feel that he is winning and I am losing. On the contrary, I'm relieved that one of us is able to serve the other and the relationship, pointing the way toward our highest potential. This is no contest. No mental "records" are ever kept, noting who provided the highest thought most often. Today, one person may be more open; tomorrow, it may be the other. And in any case, the truth is that highest thoughts nearly always "evolve" out of the communication between two people.

To come up with such a solution, the problem must be placed *outside* the couple. Both partners look at it together *from the same side*. If they find that they cannot determine together which is the highest thought, they make certain not to argue about it. Instead, they agree to separate for a while and meditate, asking for the guidance of Infinite Intelligence. They may also seek consultation with a third party who understands this technique.

In all my years of experience, I have never seen this game fail *when both parties agree to play it*. Yet I am constantly amazed at how often people forget to utilize it, even when they know it works. This can probably be attributed to old habits of choosing anger over peace. It's a habit we would do well to break. Sacred texts from all corners of the world tell us that we can only find peace by complete forgiveness. It is alarming how often we choose revenge instead.

Nearly everyone who ever hears about the Highest Thought Game asks us to give an example of how it works. So I'll focus on a very ordinary, everyday source of tension that crops up in the course of a relationship: the question of how to spend the evening. Let's say your mate wants to go bowling and would like you to go with them. You, on the other hand, want to go to the movies and you'd like them to go with you. Neither of you wants to get off your position: you dislike bowling, and they are not interested in the movie you want to see. As you probably know from experience, such circumstances often give rise to tedious bickering and low-level tension.

If you were to use the Highest Thought Game to solve this dispute, this is how you'd do it. After you both let go of your positions, you each suggest all the other possibilities.

- They could go bowling alone, or with others. You could go to the movie alone, or with others.

- You could do something totally different together that you would each like.

- You could get off your dislike of bowling and go with them tonight, and they could change their mind about the movie and go with you tomorrow night. (But *don't* do what the other person wants just to please them, then secretly resent it later.)

- You could stay home and massage each other.

- Other solutions.

Discuss each option together, determining which one would be the most fun and valuable—until *both* see one as a "win." When you've landed on the right solution, you can feel it in your body.

This technique is easy, it is fun, and it feels good. But if you still prefer attack, you will not end up making use of it. The ego wants attack and will convince you that "taking someone on" is your purpose.

Attack takes many forms besides the act of physically striking someone. We can attack anyone with words and thoughts—or with our judgments. Making our partner wrong is an attack.

A Course in Miracles tells us that if we realize that the basis of the attack is in our own mind only, we'll at least have located its source (paraphrased, text, p. 207). Once we know where the attack comes from, we can get to work putting a stop to it. As the Course says, "Where it begins it must end. For appreciation is the appropriate response" (text, p. 201) to all other human beings. "Every loving thought is true, everything else is an appeal for help" (text, p. 200), the Course tells us. When your mate is acting insanely, they are appealing for your help. You must be grateful for both their loving thoughts and their appeals for help, for even awkward pleas are capable of bringing more love into your awareness. Always try to see the situation through your mate's eyes. To practice doing this, take time right now and think of a quarrel you have with someone. Now ask yourself if you are willing to see it differently. Imagine that you are the other person, seeing it from another angle. For no one who condemns another human being can consider himself without guilt or at peace with humanity.

Taking Responsibility

When you love your mate, but still notice yourself constantly and often unfairly finding fault with her, there may be more to the matter than meets the eye. Frequently, when you find something wrong with your mate, you are actually seeing your partner as your mother, your father, or someone else in your past. Your mate then actually *becomes* that person to you, because you make them into that person unconsciously. This is a very common phenomenon; it is known as *projecting*. Because it is unconscious behavior, it may be a real trick to catch yourself doing it—but it's valuable to at least be aware of the possibility that you are projecting.

Sometimes, because of your projections, you misinterpret your partner's behavior. Other times your mate may unconsciously act out that behavior in your presence. Because you are familiar with such behavior, you've actually come to expect it, and may even "draw it out" of another person! Your mate may, in fact, start behaving like someone in your past *for* you.

In any case, your job is to take one hundred percent responsibility for *everything* that happens in your space. If your relationship is off kilter, what is your part in it? What is your case? If your relationship is stuck, you can be certain that both of you are caught in a pattern. Blame becomes a useless distraction. If you get caught in blame, you cheat yourself of the opportunity to become more enlightened. Sometimes it may look as if the problem is entirely related to your partner's case and not your own. Don't be fooled! Ask yourself, "Why do I need that kind of behavior in my space? What is my payoff?" When we take total responsibility, the truth that is revealed can be very interesting.

When couples are stuck, I recommend a marriage counseling technique that is especially effective. The process has two parts. You begin by sitting across from your mate and saying, "What really upsets me about you is _____," or, "What really bothers me about you is _____," and then completing the sentence.

The second part of the exercise begins with, "Something I really appreciate about you is _____." You then complete the sentence with *the very same answers* you gave before. The idea, of course, is for you to realize that for some reason, you in fact *wanted* these challenges in your life: perhaps to complete some lesson, become aware of some pattern, or satisfy some need. The exercise ends with both partners thanking each other for being there to reveal their patterns. Your mate really is your guru!

Keeping Your Relationships Clear with Everyone

From time to time we reach an impasse in a relationship and wonder how we should deal with it—whether to address it directly or let it alone for a while. The simple answer is that we should never allow a relationship to be "stuck," hoping that the disturbances will blow over in time. We need to do something *active* to resolve them.

Ideally, your relationship with another person should be left clear and complete at the end of each encounter. But what about the times when you realize you're uncomfortable about something that was said—but at the time of the encounter you either didn't realize the exchange upset you, or you "stuffed" your feelings instead of expressing them? If you weren't able to handle it at the time, you should immediately call the person and clear. If they left town, even if they went abroad, you can still call them. Or you may choose to write them. The important thing is to *stay with* the feeling until both of you feel good and the difficulty is resolved.

Developing the habit of getting things clear on the spot will prove extremely beneficial to your health, self-esteem, and peace of mind. Though you may feel awkward at first, after a while clearing becomes more and more natural. When someone makes a remark that causes us to feel really uncomfortable, many of us are accustomed to letting it go and then fuming later. We've been taught that this is the "polite" thing to do. A better way to handle it is to say something like, "What you just said really upsets me. I am willing to look at why and what my case is about it, but I thought I better tell you right now. Can we talk about it more until this clears?" Or if you can, ask a question such as, "Why are you doing this?" making a clear reference to the upsetting comment or action. Often, when you give other people an opportunity to explain their mindset, their position will make more sense.

When clearing, be honest. And *don't* agree with people just to make temporary peace. If you go along with something that you don't agree with, the conflict will show up later in a skewed form. You will resent having given in, and this will harm the relationship.

In the Loving Relationships Training, we do a process that helps with clearing up all types of relationships. It is important not to have old unresolved relationships on your mind—they create a psychic drain on your energy and it produces subconscious guilt. You especially need to clear your issues with your parents. At LRT, we do this through letter writing techniques such as those I mention in *Loving Relationships I.*

Because any issues you've left unresolved with your parents will come up in your current relationships, clearing with them must be done. To be honest, this is true of all old relationships; we must clean house thoroughly. As impossible as it sounds, we *can* clear all our relationships—the really old ones, the recent past ones, and the current ones. I'm talking about having *all* the relationships in your life working. It is not only possible, it is a must.

You may need to write someone you know a very unenlightened letter steeped in blame, just to get out your "charge"—and then burn it afterwards. Later you can compose a more careful version. The final letter should be one where you use "I sentences" such as, "I felt this way," rather than "blame sentences" such as, "you did that to me." The purpose of the letter should be to restore harmony, not to get even. A good screening method is to have an enlightened friend check it over to make sure the letter does not contain expressions of covert hostility. The final copy should be a letter you *yourself* would not mind receiving.

Forgiveness and Fear of Forgiveness

Forgiveness is a simple yet frequently misunderstood concept. Much has been written about it over the last two millennia, and during the past decade in particular. Forgiveness has again become the focus of a range of philosophical and practical paths that claim to promote harmonious living.

By reading a cross-section of these teachings, we broaden our conception of forgiveness and learn how to apply it to our daily lives. As you might imagine, I strongly recommend a thorough study of *A Course in Miracles*, with special attention paid to teachings specifically concerning forgiveness. As a practical aid, I'd also like to remind you of the "Forgiveness Diet" I developed in my book *The Only Diet There Is*. I originally designed the plan to help women lose weight, but it can be used as an exercise in forgiveness-consciousness as well.

Becoming conscious about forgiveness will require that you face your fear of it as well. If you find you are stuck and can't forgive— even though you have tried—you need to take a good look at your fear of forgiving. Start by saying to yourself on paper, or have a friend clear you: "The reason I do *not* want to forgive this person is____," or more importantly, "My fear of forgiving completely in this situation is____," and then finish the thought. What we so often find hidden underneath is a fear of joy and happiness. For if you forgive, *you* are the one who will have peace, joy, and happiness.

Although you may believe that you want harmony, you may be unconsciously sabotaging it, fearing it because it is unfamiliar. So, to begin with, you may need to clear your fear of joy and happiness. As strange as it may seem, many people actually believe deep down that if they are really happy, *they will die*. This erroneous idea has to be cleared first before a person will behave in a way that will promote happiness.

Quotes on Forgiveness:

From Catherine Ponder

If you have a problem, you have something to forgive. Anyone who experiences pain has a need to forgive. Anyone who finds himself in unpleasant circumstances has a need to forgive. Anyone who finds himself in debt has a need to forgive. Where there is suffering, unhappiness, lack, confusion, or misery of any sort, there is a need to forgive.

Resentment, condemnation, anger, the desire to "get even" or to see someone punished or hurt, are things that rot your soul and tear down your health. You must forgive injuries and hurts of the past and present, not so much for the other person's sake as for your own.

Hurt or hate of any kind scars the soul and works an illness in the flesh. The illness will not be fully healed while you continue to remain unforgiving.

Forgiveness begins with the one who recognizes the offense. When you get the offense out of your own heart, you have forgiven. The reconciliation which you bring about within yourself will have its effect upon your brother, and there will be an automatic forgiving on his part toward you.

Genuine forgiveness is not a casual act. The word means a "cleansing" or a blotting out of transgression. It takes time and persistence for true forgiveness to invade the subconscious levels.

You may not consciously be aware of what or whom you need to forgive in the past or present. It is not necessary that you know, though often it will be revealed to you, as you invoke forgiveness. The only requirement is that you willingly speak words of forgiveness and let those words do their cleansing work.

To forgive means to "give for" to "replace" the ill feeling, to gain a sense of peace and harmony again. To forgive literally means to "give up" that which you should not have held onto in the first place.

If only one person will dare to forgive, the problem can be solved, regardless of who else is involved and whether anyone else wants to forgive. The person who dares to forgive gains control of the situation. You may not have appeared to have any prior power to solve the problem. But suddenly there will be a change. The person who forgives will find a divine solution appearing.

You must forgive if you want to be permanently healed. Health cannot be accepted by a body that is filled with the poisons generated by unforgiveness.

When your good is delayed, that is the time to forgive. Forgiveness can sweep aside all that has delayed you in your race toward good.

If Jesus had not dared to say on the cross, "Father, forgive them for they know not what they do," he could not have experienced resurrection.

Forgiveness is all powerful. Forgiveness heals all ills. Forgiveness makes the weak strong. Forgiveness makes the cowardly courageous. Forgiveness makes the ignorant wise. Forgiveness makes the mournful happy. Forgiveness can unblock whatever has stood between you and your good. Let it.

From Gandhi

Forgiveness is the glue of the universe.
Forgiveness is the might of the mighty.
Forgiveness is the quiet of the mind.

From A Course in Miracles

The unforgiving mind is full of fear and offers love no room to be itself.

The unforgiving mind is sad without the hope of respite and release from pain.

The unforgiving mind is torn with doubt, confused about itself and all it sees.

The unforgiving mind is afraid to go ahead, afraid to stay.

The unforgiving mind does not believe that giving and receiving are the same (workbook, p. 210, 211).

The illusion is that there is something to forgive. Those who forgive are thus releasing themselves from illusions, while those who withhold forgiveness are binding themselves to them. Forgiveness is the means by which illusions disappear (paraphrase, workbook, p. 73).

Through your forgiveness does the truth about yourself return to your memory. Therefore, in your forgiveness lies your salvation (workbook, p. 103). Forgiveness is acquired. It is not inherent. Forgiveness must be learned (paraphrase, workbook, p. 210).

Forgiveness is the key to happiness (workbook, p. 211).

You who want peace can find it only by complete forgiveness (text, p. 11).

All forgiveness is a gift to yourself (workbook, p. 103).

The holiest of all the spots on earth is where an ancient hatred has become a present love (text, p. 522).

Taking Care of Your Relationship

What do you do when your body starts acting up or breaking down, or gets a sore, a pain, a fracture, an infection? As you know, the wisest course of action is to take care of it *right away*. What happens if you don't? Chances are, your body won't heal. What if you still don't pay attention? It may very likely get worse and worse until you have a full-blown disease. If, on the other hand, you are careful to heal each problem as it comes up, you can stay healthy. Your body can work. And if you live a healthy lifestyle, eating well, preventing pains, illnesses, and tensions, that is even better. You are enjoying the *vitality* of life. You master your own body and feel great.

Now let's consider *your relationship* in the same way. If you get perturbed at your mate, or upset with the relationship, but don't deal with the problem right away, your anger becomes suppressed. If even more resentment piles up on top of the first disagreement, tension builds up. The relationship quickly becomes unhealthy. By neglecting to take care of the "little things," you accumulate poisons in your relationship as you do in your body—and eventually it gets diseased. Left untreated, your relationship grows sicker. By the time you try to get emergency help it may be too late—the disease has become habitual. Through bitterness, hatred, and attack, it spreads. Soon hostilities run rampant, the damage appears irreversible. It seems impossible to fix. Separation seems the only way out, for the relationship is dead.

After listening to this all-too-frequent scenario, isn't it quite clear that you need to take the time to clear even the *smallest* problem in your relationship? It may sound like work, but what is the alternative? And does processing it *have* to be work? Not if you know clearing techniques that are fun. It can all be part of a practical new way of living in which you're clearing your relationship and your body, too, moment by moment.

In healing your body, I would *not* automatically advise you to turn it over to a standard drug-and-hospital-oriented Western medical institution, which can be so dispiriting. Nor would I advise you to turn exclusively to traditional marriage counseling or expensive psychotherapy when caring for your relationship. As new concepts for holistic health are emerging in modern medicine, so new concepts are emerging in relationship therapy. However, the emphasis in Western medicine today is finally moving in the right direction. As Dr. Deepak Chopra points out in his book, *Quantum Healing*, medical institutions are at last stressing the healing potential *within* the patient. In other words, the patient himself becomes the physician. In the same way, partners in a couple can learn how to heal their relationship within the relationship itself.

For most of us, our formal education offered no guidance in healing ourselves or our relationships; we cannot look to our schooling for help in these important areas. Instead, we must learn from Infinite Intelligence, others who are more experienced, New Age research—from anywhere possible. The most important principle is to be constantly aware of our need for knowledge and constantly open to learning and correcting ourselves.

The first step in recovering this knowledge involves getting out of denial. How many people deny the truth that their bodies are breaking down or that their relationships are troubled? Denial leads to suppression. Suppression leads to illness and death, misery and divorce. I've met people who walk around in pain every day of their lives, and because they believe that pain is "normal," they do nothing about it. I know couples who quarrel all the time, and they believe that fighting is "normal," so they do not change. Soon enough, one partner will have an affair and the other is "shocked"—though all the signs were there if any attention had been paid. The same holds true for physical illness. What I'm saying is this: when we're dealing with our relationships and our bodies, we *must* look at the *writing on the wall*. We must identify what is off balance right now and handle it before it is too late.

This advice may sound like nothing more than simple, common sense. But it's often wise to rely on your common sense and act on it. How committed are you to living fully, one hundred percent of the time? Are you actually more committed to mediocrity, suffering, suppression, pain, lack of joy, and failure? My hunch is that you would prefer joy, excellence, and pleasure. Once you get a taste of how it feels to live a cleaned-up life, you won't want to tolerate the old way of living much longer.

Another healthy way to help keep your relationship alive and in great shape is to say what you want instead of complaining about what you don't have (a tactic which can lead to chronically unhealthy communication). Staying in the positive, you and your mate can then work together to achieve your desires. It is far more effective to say, "I would really like it if we could go out together alone at least once a week," than to say, "You never spend enough time with me."

Remember your relationship lives by the same rules your body does: If you mistreat your body rather than give it what it wants and needs, it will eventually break down. So will your relationship. If you treat it with the care it deserves, you will surely reap the benefits.

Past Lives and Karma

At times, our actions during our previous incarnations, or *past lives*, exert an extraordinarily strong influence on our present relationships—and may override even skillful efforts to resolve problems in the now.

It will be very important to respect these forces when they do arise, for at these times, correction may feel beyond our control. Because of this, learning about how your past lives affect relationships can yield valuable information. Two books, *Other Lives, Other Selves* by Dr. Roger Woolger and Dick Supter's *We Were Born Again to Be Together,* are a good place to begin. Psychic Edgar Cayce's work in this area is also excellent.

The law of karma defines the character of each incarnation and provides the key to understanding the present. Linda Goodman's *Star Signs* contains some of the best writing I have found on this subject. The chapter entitled "Deja Vu" and another that addresses physical immortality are especially valuable.

Karma is the "totality of a person's actions in any one of the successive states of his existence, which determines his fate in the next." Its scientific parallel is the law of cause and effect: for every action there is a reaction. Consider what it means, for example, if someone steals from you. According to the law of karma, you can be sure that during a relationship in a former existence, *you stole from someone*, most likely the same person who is robbing you today. Linda Goodman tells us that reincarnation and the law of karma offer a clear explanation for the differences between the healthy and the sick, the poor and the wealthy. In personal relationships, the same forces are at work.

> *John hurts Mary, and Mary [in a future existence] meets John in a new body, with a different name [sometimes a different sex], and hurts John back, through a dim [subconscious] awareness that he formerly hurt her. Then comes a new lifetime for both, and now it's John's turn to hurt Mary again—then Mary's to hurt John—with each becoming the channel for the other's boomerang Karma in a chain of dreary, seemingly endless lives [incarnations].*

What a boring cycle of existence! Especially when it is so clear that this chain can be broken if either Mary or John—or both of them— get enlightened. Linda Goodman contends that either the potential giver of the karma or the potential receiver can radically alter the pattern. Keep this idea in mind when difficulties arise in your own relationship. If your partner behaves toward you in a way that you feel is unforgivable, try thinking about it this way. You must have injured or harmed that person before, and may therefore deserve this treatment.

Karma plays an equally important role in positive events. And this means that, should you receive financial support, compassion, or kindness, you *also* deserve this—you must have performed the same services for the individual who is now your benefactor during a former existence.

Our karma not only comes back to us from past lives, it affects us constantly, all the time, everywhere. Linda Goodman tells us that the concept of karma is not some kind of imagined hocus pocus; rather, it is based solidly on Newton's Law. Karma is also a spiritual law, echoed in Jesus's words, "Do unto others as you would have them do unto you."

A recent experience in my own life reveals the effect of karmic law. On a trip to Madrid last year I was in pain and was totally healed by a gifted blind physical therapist. He agreed to come in on a Sunday to work on me. On top of seeing me on his one day off, he also refused to charge me for his services. His touch was absolutely amazing. While I was dressing, I tried vainly to imagine why he would not charge me. As I was about to leave, I suddenly flashed on a connection—something from years before. Back when I was in college, I had read to the blind as a public service in my free time. I had never given my actions a thought again until that day in Spain, years later, but all at once, the physical therapist's generosity made sense.

You can work out your karma in creative ways and prevent severe damage to yourself. In her book, Linda Goodman related the remarkable story of a man who contracted a rare and incurable disease. He was told the illness would eventually paralyze him completely. Clearly an enlightened individual, he accepted his condition as an aspect of his karma, realizing that he must have caused people to be paralyzed in other lives. He began offering his services freely to disabled children and later resigned from his job to do so full time. After several months of diligently performing these services, his symptoms completely disappeared. As can be imagined, baffled doctors were amazed at his apparent "spontaneous remission." But for us, what is most important is the fact that he took *full responsibility* for what he created.

Linda says that the one instant and all-encompassing way to break the karmic chain is to forgive everyone who hurts you, even before they ask, and even if they never ask. This act in itself constitutes spiritual purification, which releases us from the endless cycle.

Review

1. Learn to recognize when your relationships are stuck.

2. Use spiritual purification methods to clear yourself.

   • Write down your negative thoughts and get them out.

   • Write a letter to God confessing your case.

   • Become comfortable using clearing methods described in the book *Pure Joy*.

3. Make a habit of clearing with everyone on the spot or as soon as possible. Be aware of the guidelines for clearing relationships.

   • Either the person who is stuck asks for help, or their partner gets their permission to help.

   • If you are the person supporting, just be there for your partner, don't do the work for him.

4. Remember that each person in a relationship should have his or her own support system outside of the relationship.

5. When you cannot clear a relationship using the techniques suggested, seek a third party or mediator.

6. Always go for solution.

7. Always practice the game of going for the highest thought.

8. Be aware of when you are projecting and take responsibility for it.

9. Learn couple counseling techniques. Remember that the very thing that bothers you about your mate is the very thing you should appreciate.

10. Always practice forgiveness. When there is someone you do not want to forgive, find out what your fear of forgiving is about.

11. Take care to "fix" each little chink in your relationship in the same way that you take care of your body to prevent disease.

12. Learn about past lives. Be aware that your past lives may be interfering with your relationships right now.

13. Understand the law of karma. Learn how you can break the chain of karma.

· PART V ·

Crises and Changes

The Death Urge in Relationships

The death urge is the secret or suppressed wish to die. It is not a natural urge, but one created in the human mind. In my other books I have written about the unconscious urge to die and how it can affect us physically: the body will quite literally self-destruct if this urge is not dealt with directly. In addition, this same impulse can affect your personal interactions, "killing off" your relationships if you aren't careful.

The unconscious death urge originated eons ago when we decided we were separate from God. All disharmony stems from this separation, which is the ultimate self-punishment. The concept of separateness is also an integral part of the belief system that considers death is inevitable.

The death urge can be a side effect of religious, family, and societal programming on death or our actual experiences with the death of a loved one. It may stem from our anger and rejection of life or a combination of these. The urge to die is present in any anti-life thought. It may manifest itself in an obvious way, or it may assume the disguise of religious doctrine—for example, the belief that heaven is elsewhere—so that death becomes desirable or attractive.

A Course in Miracles sees death as a result of "a thought called the ego," just as life springs from "a thought called God" (text, p. 388).

God did not create death; *we* did. We have nurtured it with lifetimes of accumulated negative thinking.

From early childhood we've been told about our *soul's* potential immortality. The idea that our body also has the potential to regenerate itself is never mentioned, even though Jesus *does say* "The power of life and death are in the tongue." Because we have the ability to live forever, all death is actually suicide. I cover this subject of physical immortality at length in my book *How to Be Chic and Fabulous and Live Forever* and recommend that you read it. Here, however, I want to discuss the death urge and how it affects our relationships.

Most people slowly kill themselves each day simply by indulging in the thought "death is inevitable." Once established in our minds, this idea gets projected onto our relationships with others, as well. Because of this, every couple must go through what we call the "death urge of the relationship" sooner or later. We can see this process in action; either one or both of the partners insidiously destroys the relationship—often without even knowing it. Though the partners may or may not be aware of these destructive acts, a conscious third person observing the pair can point out many ways in which the couple is killing the relationship off.

Some individuals act out the death urge within their own bodies, creating illnesses. Others act it out by sabotaging their careers. Some act it out in their relationships, tearing them apart. And some people act it out in all three areas, demolishing everything they have.

It is not difficult to figure out when your own death urge is surfacing. Things just start dying on you. Your plants may wither, pets may grow old, your appliances begin to fall apart, your car breaks down, your body may go nuts, and you may also feel depressed, moody, or really sick.

Occasionally, none of these symptoms appear because you have suppressed your urge to die. You may be the kind of person who acts your death urge out in one area only—your relationships. People who operate in this way generally have a hard time making it through when their death urge shows up. Their bonds suffer and disintegrate. Others have learned better ways of coping. If you catch the death urge as it surfaces and do something about it, you can delay the danger until help is available. At this juncture, it would be advisable to take or review the LRT, the Couples Program, the Spiritual Retreat, the Six Month Program, the India Quest, or any of the seminars that you can manage. Also, I would recommend really diving into *A Course in Miracles*. You need spiritual purification during this time and you need to stick with it!

In our daily interactions, there are a number of ways that we kill off the vitality of our relationships. These can be corrected if we are vigilant.

Not being in present time

Not being spiritually awake or nourished

Buying into prophesies of doom

Failing to express our creativity

Expressing constant put downs and disapproval

Failure to forgive

Stuffing our feelings

Addictions

Stuffing food, getting fat

Control and dependency

Giving our power away

Some relationships that survive the death urge frankly shouldn't. At times, divorce is actually a positive move. When a partnership has become spiritually bankrupt, it may be time to give it up. And, obviously, if you or your children are being harmed psychically or physically, you must consider separation.

As a rule, divorce is a personal decision. Even as a counselor, I am not the one to decide if people should stay together or not. When I see couples who are in doubt, however, I do usually offer a special prayer: "I pray for this relationship to be healed or something better for both of us." This way, either decision is a win.

There *are* times when a relationship is already dead by the time a couple seeks help, and the partners simply don't have enough desire to resurrect it. But more often I see that people really do want to stay together and are simply coping with the death urge of their relationship. If so, we can help them through it.

If you and your partner truly want to be together, yet it feels like your relationship is dying, you should definitely consider talking with someone who understands how the unconscious death urge operates. I would recommend that you see a rebirther or consultant who has already done clearing on his own death urge and has some knowledge about death. Ideally your consultant or rebirther should understand physical immortality and know that death is not necessary. Just being in the presence of an immortalist will remind you that out of the great light of God came the spark that was human life. This spark has the same energy and intelligence and power as God. You can recapture that spark and you can renew your life urge. And Infinite Intelligence can help you to illuminate your relationship once again.

This is the time you really need help to draw on that inner power, that eternal godly power, returning to a state of harmony with your inner guidance. Such rebalancing often happens during meditation or right in the middle of your rebirthing session. I have seen people pump out tons of negative energy from their death urge in one such session.

Allow those around you—plant, animal, and human—to live. And allow your relationships to live as well. Constantly give yourself the freedom to increase the vitality in your body and in your relationships, and do so with clear principles.

I remember once being on a spiritual retreat in Egypt, part of which included a cruise up the Nile by boat. Along the way, we stopped and visited very ancient temples that were extremely powerful. One of the couples on the trip, who I liked very much, started going through a difficult time. Everyone was going through difficulties, in fact, three-quarters of the people on board had diarrhea. I felt that the retreat and the temples themselves were processing everyone. The man of the married couple got up one morning and told me he and his wife were finished. He said they were complete. They had ended this cycle and that was it. I noticed that at no time did he ever say, "I want out of the relationship." Yet he was telling me they were about to divorce. I went to get one of the other trainers who was on the boat with me. We spent several hours processing with the husband and helping him get clear. His wife got very sick. I knew it was her death urge surfacing. I knew them both very well and I felt like they could make it past what they were going through at the present. Another female trainer and I went to the wife's room and laid on the bed with her. We were able to talk to her about her family patterns. Because both husband and wife reached out and because we were all there for each other, the crisis cleared and the couple are doing great now, several years later. This is the absolute beauty about being in a caring community. In the Loving Relationships Training family, the Ohana, we all help each other through crises like this. It is so much faster and easier (and less expensive) than other forms of therapy. If the couple had split up that week just because their cases were really up, it would have been very sad because they had (and still have) a beautiful marriage and they are both absolutely great.

In mortal relationships where both people are convinced that death is inevitable, their union is governed by fear, urgency, mistrust, and the constant worry, "When is this person going to die and leave me?" When both parties are working on the elimination of their death urges and are becoming immortals, relationships improve dramatically. Immortal relationships are governed by love, safety, joy, trust, and abundance of time. There is a pervasive sense of well-being and a magic that is undeniable.

When two people know that the choice to keep living is theirs, then unlimited possibilities unfold. But you really have to *want* immortality to attain it. You have to *want* to break the cycle fueled by anti-life thought patterns. If your life isn't working, you'll have no desire to live forever, yet the reason you're life *isn't* working is that you're *not* convinced that you really want to live!

Some of us simply cannot stand the possibility of physical immortality because we cannot bear the excitement—even though we may say we want an exciting life. What path will you choose? The options are there, but the decision is your own.

Certain Times, Certain Dates

Last May, one of my girlfriends who is always exuberantly "upbeat" came to visit me. She was chatting about her upcoming birthday when all at once she felt exhausted and drained of energy. I knew that around birthdays, one's birth trauma often surfaces in a powerful way, but somehow, my friend's reaction felt different. What's more, she had been a rebirther for ten years and had successfully resolved her own birth trauma. Convinced that her exhaustion must have come from a different source, I decided to question her further—from another angle. "What happened to your mother," I asked her, "when she was the age you are now going to be?" Startled, she answered, "My mother stopped having sex. She has never had it since. My father had an affair, and my mother totally changed. She began aging very rapidly." Then she went on to confess that she had been very frightened in the last weeks that her boyfriend was going to begin seeing other women.

I spoke for a short while, calmly reminding her that she did *not* have to duplicate her mother's life history; she could guide her own life in the direction *she* wished. Following our five minute conversation, her mood completely changed. She came right back to her high-energy self! Yet what if we had we not had this unexpected conversation? And what if she had not reached the conclusion? She could have easily been sucked into the unconscious pattern of setting up her boyfriend to leave her and go off with another woman. Even if he did not leave, she might have given up sex without knowing why. She might have also started aging rapidly. I have seen such reactions over and over again.

It's important to be conscious of the tendency to repeat the life history patterns of family members triggered by particular ages and dates that have made an impression on us. If a relative died and you have not resolved your feelings about their death, you may start feeling very strange at the time of year of that relative's death. You may become extremely sad or sick or lose all your energy. You may unconsciously start "killing off" significant relationships. Paranoia may cause confusion in yourself and your love relationship.

Because January was the month her father died, one of my friends went through a complete personality change every January for fifteen years! She finally got herself into the LRT six-month intensive program and cleared out this pattern. Another of our staff members had an extremely difficult year when she reached the age that her mother committed suicide. All kinds of things started dying around her. Meanwhile, the relationship she and I had became progressively more distant and troubled, coming to a head about the time of year my own sister died. Neither of us had resolved the loss of our loved one. Instead, we had transferred the loss onto our friendship, driving each other away. For her, I had become her mother; in my mind, she had become my sister.

I have described how traumatic incidents that occurred during the prenatal period and early childhood years might affect you as an adult. Now let's take this discussion a step further to see how we recreate these events after periods of time that correspond to the point in time when the trauma occurred.

Consider the case of a man who finds himself repeatedly becoming involved in what seem to be satisfying relationships, only to end them nine months later, feeling he must "escape." What can account for this peculiar pattern? Reviewing events of his birth, we learned that his birth experience was especially brutal. It is not surprising that he may tend to "break out" of his adult relationships after a period of time equivalent to the gestation period. Each time, this will reproduce the original trauma. His actions may also be confusing to him. Although he thinks that he wants to stay in the relationship, the unconscious urge to break free may put him under such pressure that he feels that he must get out of the commitment to survive. His birth thought may prove more forceful than the thought that he wants to stay, causing the breakup of his relationship.

Take a look at how long your relationships last and see if there is a pattern. If, for example, you are a woman who notices that most of your relationships end after three years, you'll need to find out what happened to you at age three to clear that incident. This is the only way to avoid getting bogged down in a "number syndrome." The incident could have been something that seems rather minor. Perhaps your father stopped letting you sit on his lap when you were three years old because he found himself getting aroused. When he said, "No," and decided to stop holding you, you may have felt very hurt, not understanding why you were rejected. Later, during adult life, when the third year of your relationship comes around, this deep sense of rejection takes on a will of its own, and you may actually *create* a man rejecting you. If this story sounds far-fetched to you, I can only say that we have seen this again and again in rebirthing and the Loving Relationships Training, and it is a lot more common than you may think. People recreate scenes and traumatic incidents over and over again until they work out the unresolved feelings surrounding those events. Numbers and dates corresponding to traumatic events trigger these incidents.

Change

Many of us are afraid of change. Perhaps we fear it because the first big transition we experience—from a liquid environment in the womb to the atmosphere—happened very quickly and we got hurt. Our birth trauma hurt us. And from these events we often adopt the mistaken idea that change hurts. We need to dispense with this idea. For when we triumph over our interpersonal problems in relationships, it also means that those relationships will change a great deal. And this kind of change is essential. It keeps us happy and vital.

The environment is rapidly transforming. How do you respond to change? How do you handle the chaos that often accompanies change—with fear, or creativity? Your fear of change comes from a need to control everything and the mistaken belief that you can. But control is an illusion that leaves us feeling rigid and isolated. The universe cannot stand still. The world won't stop revolving because you will it to. Reality moves on, and if you don't let go and change when your environment is changing, you may suffer. You mustn't hang on to the old when the new is arriving. You need to learn to *drop it*. Change is fun and exciting—even if your relationship "ends" or changes form. Remember the words of my wise friend, "*All losses are gains unrecognized.*"

The End of a Relationship

No one wants to contemplate a relationship ending—and with good reason. If you dwell on it, worry about it, or fear it, you give it energy and a separation may well occur. What you believe to be true, you create. What you fear, you attract. If you believe all relationships will end, then that is what you create.

Ending a relationship, even when you *want* it to, causes considerable pain. If you did not want the partnership to end and it did anyway, the pain may seem insurmountable. How do you get through that difficult period without intolerable pain?

As I have said many times before, if someone leaves, they are no longer the best partner for you; the universe is trying to give you something better! Nothing is taken from you without it being replaced with something better. If you remember these truths, the disappointments won't hit as hard. If you let go of the thought, "there is nobody else out there," it will be easier. You cannot receive the greater good that is coming until you let go of your attachment.

I don't like to use the term "breaking up." It seems too harsh, and, more importantly, I don't believe that relationships ever really *end*, they just change form. It is easiest to handle the potential trauma of separation by making it less of a crisis. If you and your long-time mate decide to separate, you can remain friends. It is the form of your relationship that changes. At first it may be hard to stay friends. You feel too sensitive and contact is too painful. But talk about it as a possibility for later on. If you keep your heart shut down toward someone, it hurts you. Give yourself some time to recover, but remember your mate is your teacher, your healer, and in the end, the only appropriate response toward them is gratitude. To help you along with this, I recommend that you read *A Course in Miracles*.

Remember that the failure of your relationship may actually be to your benefit. Failures can be gains not recognized: no matter what the result of your relationship was, you wanted that result! You may not be consciously aware of it, but you are always getting what you want. Even if you failed, you wanted to fail, either to reconfirm a part of your ego, to have an excuse to get angry, or to have something to blame. Because you wanted to fail, you succeeded at failing, therefore, you were really a success. Even if you don't comprehend this logic at the time, you will later, so you might as well accept it sooner! It can only ease your mind.

Staying Together or Separating

In the course of my work as a couples counselor, people sometimes ask me to tell them whether they ought to get a divorce. When this question is put before me, I must be very careful. I don't feel it is my place to tell them what to do, but it is my place to help them get clear on their own choice. As I said, most often I advise them to pray that their relationship heal *or* that something better appear for both.

Sometimes divorce is a positive sign of your going forward. For example, you may have used very poor judgment in your early years, marrying someone just like a parent whose behavior you disliked. Or you may have gotten together with someone who is your exact opposite and with whom you have little or nothing in common. If your marriage has become spiritually stagnant and there seems to be no hope of changing it, or if you realize that the partnership hinders your spiritual development, divorce or separation may then be in order.

If your relationship has merely hit a dry spell, however, or if you have simply gotten "stuck in your cases," you should try spiritual purification methods before considering a separation. It may be difficult to repair if your mate is unwilling to take the necessary steps to purify your relationship, but if God is top priority for both of you, you'll probably get through the rougher times.

Once you understand that the purpose of life is spiritual and the purpose of a union is to further spiritual expansion, you will have to reevaluate the relationship on that basis. Clearly, if the partnership is making either of you more dependent, selfish, or rigid, you are on the wrong track. But if the union purifies your ego, making you stronger, more expanded, and more spiritual, you'll very likely weather the hard parts and grow.

I've seen many people use their mate to hold themselves back spiritually. Although they may be on an enlightened path, they are committed to someone who resists enlightenment. Without realizing it, these people use their partner's reluctance as an excuse to not come forward and be all that they themselves can be. They stifle their own development to avoid threatening their mate. Time and time again, however, resentment smolders and later these same individuals wish they had had the courage to leave their relationship before so much has been invested.

Staying in a relationship that you secretly know is over, just because you are too afraid to leave, is neither kind nor virtuous. It is unfair to you and your mate. If you find yourself in this situation, get someone to help you process your fears. These fears can be erased through spiritual purification. When you separate, it is likely there may be some discomfort during a period of adjustment, but you *will* respect yourself a lot more if you are truthful to yourself and take action.

Many of us erroneously think that "there is nobody else out there" for us, or, even if there were, we would never find that person. This idea is nothing more than hogwash. There are plenty of potential mates for everyone, everywhere. You will attract new mates according to your self-esteem and the quality of your thoughts. You can easily find a new mate if you believe you can.

When a relationship ends, it is important to purify oneself and reflect. This will help avoid making the very same mistakes the next time around. I know this from personal experience. Though I would never have been able to see it at the time, I am now certain that if I had stayed in my first marriage, I would be very sick and unhappy today. The truth in my mind was not at all clear when I first married. To begin with, I was furious with God for killing my father. Everyone insisted that "the Lord took him away," and I did not want to collude with a God that killed people. My "solution" was to marry an atheist. Of course that marriage could not work because it had no spiritual foundation. But at that time I could neither trust God nor religion.

Today, much wiser for the experience, I know that if I had not gotten a divorce, there would be no LRT and I would not be the creative person I am today. I was really too young and too upset about my father's death to know the first thing about picking a mate or having a marriage work.

When I married, that first time, I was rebelling against God and trying to get as far away from him as I could. What a different person I've become. Now, the first thing I find out about a man is how *close* he is to God, and whether or not his spirituality is top priority. If it isn't, I would not be interested in mating with him. For anyone who plans to marry, as well as those who already are married, I recommend that you read *How To Spiritualize Your Marriage* by Swami Kruyananda. This book conveys the sacred joy we may find in the right union, guiding us to embrace the spirit already within us.

Letting Go Without Bitterness

Recently, I found myself thinking about an acquaintance of mine who I hadn't seen for a long time. I learned that she was still single and had not had any men in her life for a very long time. I asked a mutual friend, who I kept in close touch with, if this acquaintance was single by choice. My friend told me she was fairly certain that this woman had never recovered from her traumatic marriage and probably was just not going to get involved with a man again. I was shocked at this statement. In all the time I knew her, she had never mentioned anything about her early marriage. And we'd known each other quite a long time! The following week I ran into another woman I hadn't seen in ages. I also queried her about her relationships with men. She seemed to harbor a great deal of hesitancy, doubt, and fear about relationships. She confided to me about her marriage, which ended years before, and described its painful ending. Clearly, she had been absolutely devastated. She had gone on to raise her girls, but had never again come close to having a really intimate, healthy relationship with a man. Why? Because she had never given up bitterness.

Both of these women were avoiding relationships like the plague. They were still hurt, bitter, or afraid. The divorced mother told me that she had actually made the decision that she would never trust any man again! I felt sad about it because I could see how that idea held her back. Not only had she kept herself from creating any men because of that thought, if one did happen to show interest on his own initiative, she would not trust him. By rejecting *all* men, she may have felt she protected herself, but she was not healing herself, either. When people hang on to hurt and bitterness, it kills their aliveness and sensuality. And, ironically, this drives others even further away.

Taking a *break* from relationships to learn about yourself can be a very beneficial move. But avoiding relationships *altogether*, because you won't let yourself get over old hurts, cripples you psychically and emotionally. Here is where one must meditate on resilience. The ability to bounce back is very important in life.

Most people have created some disappointments in their life. In my own gray moments, I've gone so far as to become disappointed in myself for *creating disappointments!* But, ultimately, my faith in myself and the universe has won over. I found out that the more enlightened I became, the faster and faster I could bounce back. I realized that going ahead and taking the risk was more enlivening then holding back just because I was once hurt. In the next relationship I learned more. If it ended, I created much less hurt. The most important goal is to keep growing.

I would like to relate to you a very special story about how my Master, Babaji, helped me to learn to recover from hurt relationships—and this was before I even met him! I now realize that I had been with him before in another life that I did not remember. In any case, the story takes place in this lifetime at a time when I had been called to India.

At the time I first planned to go to India, I was a newly certified rebirther having a great relationship with another rebirther. My partner had become a trainer with me, and we traveled together working as a team. We had been involved with each other for two years, when one day he came home and simply said to me, "I have to leave." I was shocked. I had thought we were getting along very well. I asked him, "Why? Are you upset with me?" And he answered, "No." "Are you upset with our relationship?" Again, he said, "No." Then he said, "I just have to leave." And so he did. No explanation was given and I never saw him again. That same week other things began to go wrong, as well. A friend wrecked my sports car and left it lying in a ditch. And on top of that, the beautiful home I had been living in was suddenly sold and I was informed that I must vacate immediately. I had lost everything I was attached to.

Though I was trying to be enlightened and to "handle it," in truth, I was very shaken. For days I felt as if my feet never really touched the ground. The shock entirely erased my travel plans from my mind. Then, one morning after yet another night of fitful sleep, I woke up and I remembered that I was going toward India. "Oh, I get it," I thought. "I have to go to the Master, naked, without attachments." All the losses I'd just experienced finally made sense. Calmer now, I pulled myself together and left for Asia.

Weeks later, walking along in New Delhi, I found myself painfully yearning for my former partner. Indulging in my loneliness, I only made myself miserable. Then, suddenly, without knowing where it came from, I heard a voice—the voice was part of a "presence" I felt to the right of me. It asked, "What if leaving could be a joy?" "That is ridiculous!" I cried. I could not imagine such a thing. But as much as I resisted this presence it seemed only to grow. Finally, it spoke again,"Just wait until you see what I have for you next!" I was so startled that I fell to the ground, humbled. I wept and finally spoke in a whisper, "Pardon me for my little faith." Rising, I left to the Himalayas where I would come to understand everything.

It was only later that I learned the voice I had heard in the streets of New Delhi was that of Babaji. He was reminding me that when something or someone leaves us, it is no longer best for us, and that nothing is taken from us without it being replaced by something better. Babaji taught us that *faith is everything*. Later, I was given *so much* beyond my former life.

If a relationship ends and you feel dispirited because you did not want it to be over, it may be valuable to do a truth process completing a sentence such as, "The reason I wanted to have this relationship end was _____." This exercise is *especially* helpful if the other person left when you wanted the bond to continue.

The truth is that "results are your guru." Even though you may not yet realize it, you *did* in fact want it to end. *A Course in Miracles* reminds us to beware of the temptation to perceive ourselves as unjustly treated. No one can hurt you but yourself!

A period of grieving is, of course, natural. But if you wish to, you can shorten the time by nurturing your self-esteem. Remember that you yourself can go out and create new relationships whenever you like. If you are a woman, you do not have to wait around for men to ask you out. (See *Loving Relationships I* for lessons on how to create mates in your life.) You can also cut down the grieving time through spiritual purification. (See *Pure Joy.*)

I believe it is important to refrain from judging yourself adversely if you have a series of brief relationships instead of fewer, longer ones. Shorter relationships are not automatically "bad." Sometimes you need people to come into your life for shorter periods. Each will be your guru for a time, followed by the next, who will also serve as your teacher. The important question is this: Have you become more loving with each new experience?

Marianne Williamson talks about various alternatives on her excellent tapes about relationships and *A Course in Miracles.* Listen to them instead of moping around. Get going on a new life. There are new people to meet, new experiences to relish, joy is around the corner. The whole idea is to create a sense of *inner joy* that doesn't depend on exterior circumstances going well.

Review

1. Understand the death urge and be very clear how it is now operating in your life. How does it affect your relationship? Are you unconsciously killing off your relationship? Get the help you need from someone who understands the unconscious death urge and relationships.

2. Support each other in the wonderful process of living forever.

3. Be aware of certain auspicious dates and times which may strongly affect you: anniversaries of traumatic incidents, deaths, divorces, or transitions.

4. Use change as a creative force. Change the thoughts that make change frightening to you. If you tend to be upset in the presence of change, practice the art of "dropping it." Stop indulging in the upset!

5. If someone leaves, know this: they are no longer the best partner for you. Something better is coming.

6. At the end of a relationship, let go of all bitterness. This will help you be resilient and allow something better to appear.

7. If you cannot seem to let go and you feel stuck in blame, get help, especially by doing the truth process.

8. Do not judge yourself if you have short relationships. Perhaps you need different gurus at different times. The goal is to become more loving with each one.

· PART VI ·

Relationships and Daily Living

Outside Friendships

It is both healthy and enlivening to have close friendships with people other than your mate. How much room does your relationship allow for outside friendships?

A Course in Miracles strongly discourages us from cultivating a "special relationship"—loving one person exclusively, holding that person above all others, above ourselves, and even above God. The Course tells us that the special relationship is the ego's chief weapon to keep you from God (paraphrase, text, p. 317) and you cannot enter into real relationships with any of God's Sons unless you love them all equally. Love is not special (paraphrase, text, p. 247).

Depending on one person to satisfy *all* of your needs puts tremendous pressure on your partner. Close, intimate, non-sexual friendships with others can take some of the "heat" off your relationship. You'll have to be sure, of course, that you do not use these friendships as a secret weapon—or as an escape valve which enables you to avoid dealing with important issues in your main relationship. Also, you will need to know how to skillfully and consciously handle jealousy, competition, and time factors. These skills may require some practice and experience—but they *can* be acquired.

Outside relationships round us out and allow our relationship to breathe. In doing so, it prevents the kind of rigid limitations that no healthy individual can adhere to.

We need to recognize that love is abundant, not some finite resource that must be sparingly distributed. Let's remember that if we actually reached the level of consciousness to which we aspire, we ultimately could and should be in love with everyone.

Money and Relationships

Conflicts over money rank as one of the most frequent causes of divorce. This news comes as no surprise to most of us, for we know from experience that money is indeed easy to fight about. In any case, money conflicts differ in essence very little from any other kind. The ego loves conflict. When we give up the addiction to conflict and the desire to get rid of peace, we become willing to stop fighting about everything, including money. Even issues concerning finances can be resolved peacefully.

Where do we begin solving money conflicts? Each person must start by handling their own "money case." That includes all the negative conditioning each of us has had about money—conditioning that has affected everything from a lack of prosperity to our addiction to greed and overspending.

My own opinion is that you can take all kinds of seminars on money, read any number of books, and learn a whole range of methods to handle it, but if you do not process your own emotional blocks about money, even the most refined tools and techniques won't work. Or, if they appear to solve your present problem now, chances are you will later sabotage or blow your financial gains anyway.

When you get too entangled in the material world without first establishing the proper consciousness for what you have, the imbalance can cause chaos and disaster. What kind of imbalances can come about? On one end of the scale there is *greed* and on the other end of the scale there is what we call a *money rejection complex*. Neither of these extremes will bring you happiness. What you want is a reasonable balance.

Greed is an uncontrollable, insatiable appetite for more than you need. Although the person afflicted by greed has no apparent reason, he thinks he must have more and more and more. He strives for it constantly. Greed usually stems from competitive thinking, the idea that one must be better and possess more than another in order to feel worthwhile. Yet, ironically, while accomplishing or acquiring more, the greedy person senses only a greater emptiness, a void which in turn fuels a yearning for even more property. The cycle goes on and on. As my friend Constance said, you will never be satisfied while you are ruled by greed.

At the other end of the spectrum, a "money rejection complex" stems from the belief that money is sinful or bad, and you therefore block the receipt of money. You will never be satisfied while such thinking persists. Why? Receiving is not selfish. It is simply a completion of a cycle of energy. In the Loving Relationships Training, we talk about money being *innocent*. It is really just paper and energy. Your own energy determines whether or not money flows freely to you. The higher your energy, the more money you can attract and handle. Because your own energy regulates this flow, only you can deprive yourself, and all you receive is up to you, as well. Decide that you will receive what you are worth. Learn to think in an unlimited way in general, not just thinking big, but thinking creatively.

As we develop higher spiritual qualities, we change our vibrations. We can make our vibrations magnetic. The task is to become happy first. If we are unhappy with one aspect of our life, it may affect all others. If you truly desire abundance, each area of your life must work. If you are confused about money and spirituality and do not believe the two can operate simultaneously, you had best review your belief systems about God. God is opulent! God is omnipresent wealth!

John Randolph Price, author of *The Abundance Book*, explains that God does not provide us with money or homes—he gives us Himself. He gives us *divine substance*, and substance becomes money and homes. This substance, or creative energy, flows through the mind of human beings and externalizes itself as a mirror of our thoughts and convictions. Money, he explains, is an *effect*, a by-product of this process. When we concentrate on the effect, we often forget the cause. As we lose sight of the cause, the effect begins to diminish. When we focus our attention on *getting* money, we actually shut off our supply.

The upshot is this: if you truly wish to increase your wealth, you must this very moment cease to believe that money is your support, your security, or your safety—money isn't, God is! When you understand and realize this truth, an uninterrupted supply will give rise to abundance. You must look to God alone as the source. Do you want more money, more prosperity in your life? Then transform your consciousness from one of effects—materialism—to one of cause—spirituality.

There are many useful books on money and prosperity consciousness. We sell a number of them in our community. If you call any LRT center we can recommend both classic guides as well as important new contributions to the field.

In a couple, each partner should know thoroughly the financial habits of their own and their mate's family. Mates should help each other to overcome feeling "stuck" rather than clinging to blame.

In their book *Money, Sex and Communication*, Phil Laut and Jeanne Miller describe a wonderful process for couples who want to improve their communication about money. Starting off the exercise, partner A says to partner B, "Describe your family's financial life." B answers. The following questions prompt B to elaborate further:

- Who made the money?

- Who made decisions about its value?

- How did you get money?

- How did you feel about their work?

- What did they tell you about money?

- What were family arguments about money?

- What were the opinions about the rich and the poor?

When B's account is complete, the partners switch roles and B asks A the same questions.

Many of us believe that we know all we need to know about our mate's views about money. But focused questioning may reveal that our partner's attitudes diverge greatly from what we imagined. This information is crucial because these very attitudes dictate financial decisions affecting both partners.

Too often, money is a taboo subject. Laut and Miller suggest regular, weekly meetings where partners discuss financial affairs, including current agreements, money goals, bills, future economic prospects, savings, fears, and feelings. So if you are fighting about money, stop *now*. What good will that accomplish? Anger blocks money. Guilt blocks money. Sitting down calmly and approaching financial issues in a sober, concerted way diffuses the tension and clears space for other interests. I certainly wish this had been done in my family when I was a child.

It's tempting to look the other way when it comes to the nitty-gritty aspects of our financial affairs. Do you balance your checkbook regularly? Do you make extraordinary purchases on an ordinary budget? Have you "maxed out" a collection of credit cards? Can you distinguish your own financial patterns from your mate's? Are you using a joint bank account to obscure this? The important point in all this is to get a clearer picture of how you use your financial energy.

The most important of all to your inner presence or higher self is the money maker. The God Presence in you provides for your welfare. If you acknowledge that, you will keep on track with money matters. Focus on the lavish abundance of Divine Substance in the whole world.

Personal and Global Greed

What does it really mean if our finances are a mess? If you happen to decide that you simply don't want to think about money, why should it be anyone else's business? The answer is not so very hidden. Each day, each one of us will have to face the fact that we are creating a world based on materialistic greed. It is a fixation. We are like addicts.

Jose Arguelles, the master of planetary transformation who created Harmonic Convergence in 1987, has said that the higher beings laugh at us because we ignore the fact that *we are the cancer of the earth*. We cannot understand that worldwide crises like pollution, cancer, dying species, terrorism, and the depleting of the ozone layer all express our collective addictions. Jose asserts these global crises stem from materialistic greed. As human beings became increasingly involved in creating material wealth for ourselves, we became further and further separated from our light bodies, and create the age of darkness. We can get help for ourselves in combating this addiction, he contends, but first we must let go of our denial and arrogance and realize outside help is necessary.

In his book *Surfers of the Zuvuya*, Jose describes our tragic fate should we refuse to change our path. He urges all of us to join Earthlings Anonymous (E.A.), an international organization whose covenant declares: "We admit we are powerless over our habits and the disempowering institutions we created to support them." As this manifesto suggests, we're only powerless if we are in our ego, the part of our mind that won't let go, and is in opposition to God's will, which is the true "Controller." Our God-Self can lead us to clean up our act on the planet.

Guilt

Guilt is not only ungodly, it is an attack on God. If you assail God-Self with guilt, you will surely end up punishing yourself, for guilt demands punishment. Take a good look at your life. Are you punishing yourself in your career? Your financial dealings? Your personal relationships? Your body? All of these areas?

In the Loving Relationships Training we have observed a common guilt pattern. Because many of us tend to believe that we've done something wrong or that there is something inherently wrong with us, we don't think we deserve the love we desire. And we often subconsciously sabotage the love we do receive. This pattern holds true in relation to money and success as well. If we do not believe that we deserve to be rich, we will either keep money away from ourselves or blow it when we do receive it.

Guilt can destroy your happiness and your relationship very quickly. If you feel guilty, you'll feel like you don't deserve your mate's love. You may suppress this guilt long enough to get *into* the relationship, but it cannot be held down forever. As soon as you make a commitment, guilt will very likely resurface, and you will find yourself rejecting the love of your mate. You may push your partner away outright—or you may invalidate them by suspecting their love for you is not genuine. In either case, you will force them to leave.

The seeds of guilt can begin to develop as far back as your own conception. Having taken on a body, you may feel guilty for thinking that you are separate from God. If you don't resolve this painful feeling, you will punish yourself your whole life long, finally creating your own death. Perhaps you may experience another type of guilt— what we call the "Infant Guilt Syndrome," characterized by a feeling of intense guilt for having hurt your mother at your birth. In addition, you may harbor religious guilt, social guilt, and guilt for all your wrongdoings. You may even be carrying guilt from past lives.

The only way to escape guilt is through forgiveness. In its final, desperate attempt to maintain control over the ego, guilt will demand that you think you are guilty for daring to think you are innocent.

Take the case of a rather kind person who has no objective reason to harbor guilt feelings. This woman told me she was afraid to let go of guilt because if she did, she "might do something bad." I tried to explain to her that she had it backwards. Believing you were born a sinner makes you unconsciously want to destroy yourself. In this way, her guilt was forcing her to unconsciously do things she would feel guilty about. Realizing she is innocent will guarantee that she will act in an upright manner that will enable her to *feel* innocent.

Sex

As we are all aware, sexual problems also constitute a major cause of divorce. *I Deserve Love*, the first book I wrote, focuses on resolving conflicts in this area. Even though there were already a great number of books on sex being published at the time, I wrote my own because I did not feel any of the publications at the time really addressed the *cause* of sexual dysfunction. In *I Deserve Love*, I put forward the idea that the cause of sexual problems is always a negative thought in the ego's thought system. The book is just as popular now as it was when it first came out. As I concluded then, all that matters is this: *Are you in the Holy Spirit's thought system about sex or the ego's thought system?*

Though some people still ignore the warnings, almost everyone in our country is now at least aware of the health risks associated with casual sex. But I wonder if people are aware of the fact that casual sex can actually devitalize you—aside from the question of disease. I have heard spiritual teachers explain that when two people have sex for purely physical reasons, we can literally exchange dangerous psychic shock waves that disturb our spiritual recharge. If you don't have the right magnetic recharge taking place, an imbalance of this energy is discharged. The more you have sex in such circumstances, the more the imbalance expands.

Over time, it became clear that we needed another book, one that would describe how birth trauma affects sexuality. It seemed most appropriate for an experienced rebirther to write it. I also felt that an LRT trainer should write it—one who understood relationship technology.

In the end, the person I approached was Rhonda Levand, a trainer who had a keen interest in the topic. Rhonda's wonderful book, *Sexual Evolution*, is exactly what was needed. An essay of Rhonda's appears in Part II of this book.

When you are with your true mate and truly in love, understanding the holiness of that instant and remaining in the Holy spirit's thought system, your whole being is illuminated with cosmic grace. Revitalization takes place. Holy sex reunites us with our true self. When your mind and heart are pure and you offer your sexuality to the Holy Spirit, the opportunity for the cosmic ecstasy of God suddenly arises.

Have you ever considered studying Tantra sex, both an ancient discipline and a spiritual system? Look into *New Age Tantra Yoga*, by John Zitko, and *Tantra: The Art of Conscious Loving*, by Charles and Caroline Muir. In the Tantric teachings, sexual love represents a sacrament—its ultimate goal is union with God. These teachings elevate your sexual relationship to the level of art, according to the Muirs. In addition, Zitko contends, you and your mate can use Tantra to achieve physical immortality together!

Your Space and Environment

How Does Your Environment Support Your Relationship? During the Loving Relationships training, people often laugh at how adamant I am about neatness in regards to their space. But I know from experience that neatness affects your mind and your relationship. When I visit a home, I can instantly determine a family's "aliveness quotient" and also how much they respect each other by the way the home looks. This is not a matter of finances or expensive items; the way you care for your living space reflects how you feel about yourself and those you live with.

Your home and the various spaces that comprise it offer you a clear, tangible way to measure your level of self-esteem and vitality.

Let's take the kitchen:

> *Is the stove really dirty and the cooking pots all banged up? Are handles missing? Is the food in the refrigerator moldy? Are the cupboards a mess? Are the sponges in the sink all dirty with dirty dishes stacked up? Is there birdseed all over the floor? Is the garbage overflowing?*

In the living room:

> *Are the plants dead? Have the cats scratched up all the furniture? Are the light bulbs burned out? Is the TV dominating everything?*

In the bathroom:

> *Are the towels rancid? The shower curtain molding? The mirror all splattered? Do the shower and bathtub have dirty rings? Are old bottles lying around? Is the scale rusty?*

In the bedroom:

> *Is there junk piled around? Boxes and items that are not particularly sensual? Closets bulging with old clothes that are not flattering, or clothes that are too small to be an incentive to lose weight? (That will definitely sabotage your self-esteem!)*

Why not throw open your closets and try everything on? Then look in the mirror and ask yourself, "Does this turn me on?" If the answer is no, give it away. (How do you expect your partner to be turned on if you aren't?) Always dressing nicely, even at home, enhances your mood and sensuality. It is a way a person can show appreciation for their mate. It shows them that you care about their opinion and you care enough to make them feel good by the way you look and the way the house looks.

What about your car?

Is it all banged up? Is it dirty most of the time? Is there dog or cat hair everywhere on the seats? Are there cigarette butts, gum wrappers, soda cans all around? Are there old newspapers and piles of crap on the floors of the car? Are major parts of the car not working well? Is it really an old wreck? What does this say about the way you feel about your body?

And, finally, what about your yard?

Do you realize that the whole planet is your backyard? Why not have a garage sale and get rid of junk in your place? Space and silence gives you vitality.

Naturally you want to feel relaxed in your home. Notice the difference in your mood and the vitality of your relationship when your space is pretty and neat. Maybe you need to hire a housecleaner once a week. Some people clean up household surfaces, but somehow leave *grime* everywhere underneath. If that describes how you deal with your living space, have you ever stopped to consider the idea that grime, dirt, filth, and things falling apart represent your *death urge?*

I have never understood why people don't get each thing that needs fixing fixed immediately instead of letting it go. When you let something go and don't fix it right away, you end up with a disintegrating house and broken-down belongings. In time, your home will become a depressing place and yet you will feel that fixing so many things at once is far too expensive. If you wait longer still, you end up feeling run down, and in the meantime your space will have fallen apart.

On the other hand, careful maintenance of your property and belongings propels a cycle of positive energy. When your mind is clear and your thoughts orderly, you want everything fixed. In the same way, when you fix something, you also feel like maintaining yourself and your relationships properly.

Still, a surprising number of people let their houses go until a seemingly impenetrable mess accumulates. When they finally clean it all up, the job exhausts them so much that they end up taking another break for weeks at a time. As garbage builds up again, their home becomes a mess all over again. The cycle continues needlessly. It makes much more sense to clean up everything on the spot, so your space is always neat. For the heavier work, to prevent dirt and grime, hire a cleaning service if you are able to afford one; it's not as costly as you think. If such an arrangement is definitely beyond your means, try pooling your own efforts. The whole family can work together as a cleaning team.

It could be that as a Virgo, I am extraordinarily obsessed with this topic of cleanliness and order. But, time and time again, I have seen neatness enhance some relationships and neglect erode others.

A couple has to negotiate and work out their own way of doing household chores—a way that really and truly works for both partners. What can get tricky is if one mate grew up in a home that was very neat while the other came from a home that was rather disorderly. Behavior resulting from habits learned in childhood can be a big point of contention—but solutions can still be found. Chores don't have to cause tension: it is fun and easy to work out agreements, try them out, and renegotiate them until both are satisfied.

I will tell you a true story. I once lived with a man who was much neater than I am. If you know me, this may be hard to believe, since I have always had fastidious habits. He, however, was even more particular. A complete perfectionist. He was forever polishing the glass coffee table and dishware, never allowing even *one* coffee cup to sit in the sink! I constantly felt nervous around him. I could never relax. In my eyes, he was obsessed—and of course I considered my standards "just right." After cohabitating for several months, the tension mounted inside me. Several times I almost felt like fighting with him. Luckily, I refrained, and in the end I decided I should approach the problem a bit more intelligently. One Saturday morning when he had time to talk, I sat down with him. I said, "I noticed that we have very different styles of neatness. I am having trouble doing it the way you do it, but maybe if you explain your mind-set about this subject, it will help me." When he responded he truly surprised me, "Well, Sondra, it is really very simple: Prepare every room for God." I was stunned. Between the two of us, his was absolutely the highest thought. I got off all my lower thoughts and went up to his and I asked him to help me reach his level. Our relationship taught me a great deal.

Marriage

The day my marriage ended, many years ago, the following scene occurred: on the top floor of a two-story apartment building, my husband and I sadly packed up our belongings. After seven years and many experiences together, we were moving out and parting from one another. At the very same moment, scuffling movement, easy laughter, and the thud of moving furniture could be heard from the ground floor below. A newly wed, married couple was moving into the apartment beneath us!

The irony of the situation was crushing—and not at all funny. Indeed, many jokes about marriage are very sad. As in the following anecdote, which is meant to be told as a joke. Humor acts as a weak cover for cynicism and hurt feelings.

> A lady has finished a meal in a hotel coffee shop and asks for her check. Surprised, the waitress exclaims, "But I put your breakfast on the tab of the man sitting next to you, the guy who just left!" "What made you do that?" the lady asks, "I don't even know him. I've never seen that man before in my life!" "I'm sorry," the waitress explains, "You two weren't talking to each other so I thought you were married!"

This joke actually reveals an all-too-common phenomenon. Did you know that a psychologist interviewed 40,000 married couples on communication patterns and it turned out they talked to each other on the average of only 27 *minutes a week?* What is it about marriage that so often leaves two people so alienated from one another? I've been investigating this question for many years following my divorce, and I must say that most of my findings did *not* make remarriage very appealing.

When actress Glenn Close got pregnant some time ago and moved in with her man, reporters asked her if she intended to marry. Close responded, "Why should the *government* be involved in this?" Reading her comments, I became aware that I shared Close's point of view. Yes, I decided, I might get remarried spiritually, but not legally.

During my rebellious stage that followed, I attracted a book called *A New Vision for Women's Liberation.* This book really stirred me up because it contained the most radical statements on marriage I had ever read. The author, Bhagwan Rajneesh, declared that marriage is out of date and that it destroys all possibilities for happiness. He insisted that marriage makes everyone a zoo animal, that it exacerbates the will to die and leads to prostitution. He believes that marriage is an anachronistic barrier that must disappear and that it has ruined the status of women.

Over time, I studied the subject more and more deeply, reading other books such as Swami Kruyananda's *How to Spiritualize Your Marriage,* which *advocated* marriage for another set of reasons. Gradually, I began to feel that the institution of marriage itself was not so negative. At fault were the false notions about what marriage should *mean* and the way people responded to one another once inside the marriage. In other words, marriage becomes a sacred bond only if it is *made* sacred—otherwise it is simply a social contract. The sound reasons for getting married that I read and thought about included these:

- Marriage can help a person achieve inner balance (especially between reason and feeling).

- Marriage helps break the confines of selfishness and ego, helping one to learn to live in a larger reality than one's own.

- Marriage helps one expand one's identity.

- It provides a "proving ground" for one's inner spiritual development. It tests a married mate's spiritual qualities.

- Marriage is a vehicle through which one can achieve union with God (after achieving union with the God in your mate).

Pushing ahead further, I began looking into Yogananda's teachings on marriage and came across this piece of wisdom: "The desire for marriage is universal because of the cosmic power of love to draw everything back to oneness." The guru stresses how important it is that marriage be based on divine friendship between equals with unconditional love, unconditional loyalty, and the divine qualities of "Kindness, Respect, Trust, and Faith." He prioritized the essential foundations for marriage in this way:

1. Soul unity (similar spiritual ideals and goals and a willingness to attain them through study and self-discipline).

2. Similarity of interests.

3. Physical Attraction (which soon loses its attractive power if soul unity and similarity of interest are not present).

How often people reverse these priorities and suffer because of it!

Clearly, marriage is no panacea. Matrimony itself does not solve problems. In fact, it probably accentuates existing difficulties all the more strongly. Marriage must be manifested in a spiritual context, for if your marriage becomes spiritually stagnant, divorce is likely to be the only possible resolution.

Finally, after reading all sorts of opinions about marriage, I was eager to come to some conclusions on the subject. For me, doing so was particularly difficult because I both agreed with parts of the extremely radical arguments against marriage *and* the sweet spiritual positions that favor it.

In the end, it became evident to me that it is not marriage, but rather what you *do* with marriage that determines whether you achieve liberation or delusion. Because I preferred liberation, I realized that only one question mattered: Am I into the ego's thought system with marriage, which is delusion, or the Holy Spirit's thought system, which is true reality? In other words, *is this a holy relationship or an unholy relationship?*

Let's look at a range of qualities which characterize the two types of union.

Unholy Relationship	vs	*Holy Relationship*
The ego's mind		The Holy Spirit's mind
Contacts into limited state of self-enclosure		Expands into greater realities
Guiding throught: What can I gain from the other?		Guiding thought: What can we give to one another?
Reinforces your case (negativity)		Purifies through spiritual discipline, freeing negativity in both partners
Causes clinging, fear, dependency		Trust and the freedom to be; reinforcement of self-expansion
Sees the body as sex object		Sees the body as temple of God

Ego relationship governed by:	*Spiritual relationship governed by:*
Separation	Aliveness
Conflict	Love
Fear	Harmony
Pain	Peace
Anger	Safety
Worry	Certainy
Misery	Trust
Scarcity	Happiness–Joy
Sickness	Perfect Health
Depression	Abundance
Death	Immortality

If we are sizing up a typical ego-based marriage, all Rajneesh's criticisms of matrimony in *A New Vision for Women's Liberation* would seem to be true. But if we look at a marriage that embraces the Holy Spirit's thought system, we see a very different picture. I wouldn't want you to think I am trying to get you to conform to any belief system of mine, especially on the subject of marriage; belief systems are created by human beings and are changeable. The mind of God is something else. The mind of God is a state of *being*. And I do know that if we all align with the mind of the Holy Spirit, then we are on the right track.

Children

If you are planning to have children, there is a fascinating book called *The Child of Your Dreams* that you should read long before conception. Huxley asserts that when conceiving, a spiritually compatible couple have the ability to attract highly spiritual souls. Before conception you can send out an invitation to the kind of child you want. In meditation, you welcome that child. A soul with a love for peace will be attracted to peaceful parents. I have written a book called *Ideal Birth* and suggest that you read it as well as *The Secret Life of the Unborn Child* by Dr. Thomas Verny. I want to remind you that when the child is within the womb, *whatever* you are feeling and doing is transmitted through vibration into the child.

During the last decade, remarkable headway has been made in the field of pre- and perinatal psychology. One of the most significant findings shows that imprints determining tendencies toward dysfunctional behavior in childhood and adulthood are formed during the prenatal period, from conception to birth, and during the first twelve months. This discovery contradicts the previously accepted theory that these imprints develop when the child is one to three years old. Children with reduced prenatal, birth, and perinatal trauma are generally brighter, more alert, intuitive, assertive, and creative. They exhibit independent learning patterns, are clearer about their own needs, display high self-esteem, and score measurably higher on intelligence tests. These differences have been obvious for some time to those of us who are working in the field and in rebirthing. I thank Margaret Grant, who sent me a publication called *The Dialogue On Conscious Education,* which is co-sponsored by the Pre and Perinatal Psychology Association of N.A. and the Task Force on Conscious Education. For specific information, call her at (303) 574-7028.

Child-rearing is a trying yet fascinating process. In the Loving Relationships Training, we make a point of reminding our participants that *children are our gurus.* Youngsters unflinchingly act out our subconscious thoughts, revealing our mind's inner workings. Their unfiltered reactions can teach us a great deal about ourselves and about relating responsibly. The wisest among us will take careful note of what they are saying.

As a parent, it's sometimes hard to conceive of our child's self as separate from our own. But a parent's task is exactly that. One must remember that children are already developed souls from their own past lives. Because children come as guests to their family, one should never attempt to possess a child. As Roger Woolger tells us in his book *Other Lives, Other Selves,* a child is *not* a blank slate at birth. We mustn't expect children to grow up reflecting our own desires. Nor can we afford to delude ourselves into thinking that they have everything to learn from us, or that children are simply helpless creatures. Education ought not to describe a process akin to computer programming. The true meaning of education is "drawing out" by bringing forth the wisdom our children already possess—not by imposing our own will upon them.

There are some guidelines that are especially useful when your child has a problem.

- Try not to speak from a feeling of anger.

- Try not to let your personal irritation dictate the treatment.

- Focus on how you can help him overcome it rather than how it drives you crazy.

Tara Singh offers exceptional advice for parents in her book, *How To Raise A Child Of God.*

> The child is born with his own space and with his own resources. It is the responsibility of the parent not to intrude on

that innocence by putting their own frustrations and knowings on the child. He is born with space. Let the space be.

The function of a parent is to awaken a child to his own eternity, to his own holiness, to the perfection of what God created . . . not to phony books and waste.

A child needs to play . . . mental faculties must awaken in their own internal way and should never be forced. If he is protected from being imposed upon, he will have the discrimination of his own conviction and will not violate what is true within.

It would be so good if you could take your children to a prayer or meditation room in your house . . . a spacious little room uncluttered, with a few cushions, a bowl of water, a plant, and a picture of two of Divine Beings. This room can be alive with purity of space. Take your child into this room every day and come to peace within yourselves.

Here are more of Tara Singh's lovely teachings:

Teach your child not skills, but love to share.
Teach him to have more space in his life, the richness of stillness.
Teach him to widen the gaps of silence between the thoughts with relaxation.
Teach him that all things in their origin are of the one source.
Teach him to pray for his adversary to regain his own peace and harmony.
Teach him not to be controlled by another.
Teach him to bless all things with his peace.
Teach him non-waste and the love of conservation . . . to be a friend of trees, dawn, and twilight.
Teach him simplicity and gratefulness . . . to love virtue.
Teach him to be a friend unto himself.

The purpose of parenthood is to return the child to God. To raise a child of God is to allow God to participate in their upbringing: would you like to make this civilization truly great? Would you like your children to be able to actualize that dream? Then teach your children this: that *thought is creative*. Negative thoughts produce negative results and positive thoughts produce positive results. Teach them to apply these truths to every aspect of their lives. Insist that schools teach these ideas. (Why didn't we learn that in school in first grade?)

Imagine a civilization where everyone grew up *knowing* these truths and *practicing* them! Start setting an example now. Raise the quality of your own thoughts. Clear out your negative subconscious thoughts. Help your children get to higher and higher thoughts. Let your love guide you.

My Case on Relationships

If you've read my other books, you are familiar with my case about the opposite sex. Like everyone else, I had to overcome my fears, anger, and a negative thought system that seemed insurmountable. The truth is we all have to overcome obstacles—but doing so takes time and hard work.

Many people are convinced they have the greatest disadvantages, the worst childhood. Creating a successful life depends on how we deal with these challenges. At times I felt like I had a huge handicap, having had my father die just when I was blossoming as a teenager. Yet I also knew that some women had to live with alcoholic fathers, abusive fathers, or no fathers at all.

It took me years to recover from my father's death. Until I did, I created men leaving—even those who swore they were in love with me as they walked out the door—because in my experience, men were always leaving. My dad was always leaving for the hospital. I never knew if he would return.

My father died the night before my high-school graduation, where I was to receive honors as the salutatorian of the class. At our school, the salutatorian traditionally delivered an address called "Message to the Parents." I gave that speech, but I was frozen throughout the ceremony. And though I can't recall a thing I said, I do remember that the whole audience was crying—300 people in all—the entire population of my town. Everyone I'd known since I was a small girl attended. My graduation was transformed into a painful, early funeral.

Not surprisingly, these events made a deep impression on me, one I could not stand too face. Fleeing from these painful memories, they stayed locked up in my unconscious, destined to repeat themselves over and over again. Eleven years after my high-school graduation, for example, I recreated my father's death. On the day of my graduate school commencement ceremony, my husband left. Our marriage ended or "died" on that day. At the time, I didn't make the connection between this painful loss and my father's death. But later, after I began to learn more about my own patterns, the link became clearer. This understanding also led me to realize why, as an undergraduate, I had inexplicably skipped my college graduation ceremony: graduations and completions of events had become too much for me to bear.

As many people do, I went through hell after my divorce. Feeling panicky and alone, at times I lost sense of my own self-worth. My hair fell out. Fortunately, during this period I was able to experience the miracle of rebirthing. As a result, I discovered the Human Potential Movement and began attending seminars. Step by step, I began to heal, to recover from my fall.

During this period, my personal life matched my public one. Heady with new concepts and sensations, I dove headfirst into a period of self-exploration. I had many relationships; I learned many things. Time passed. All in all, I had 20 happy years on my own as a single woman. I came to believe, in fact, that I'd mastered the art of being single. I liked it. I didn't ever want to remarry. I relished my freedom and admired single women. Naturally, I felt pleased and validated by actress Shirley MacLaine's comments in *New Woman* magazine when she said, "I'm not seeing any one man and I'm very content. I have lots of good friends, and I like that. When you get to be my age and you've been around the block a few times with love affairs, deep commitments, and live-in relationships, you realize that you don't need a man anymore to satisfy your existence. I'm really with my freedom and my friends all over the world."

I appreciated what MacLaine said. She expressed my feelings exactly. I was certain that I could go on forever living the same way and be satisfied. Even when people gave me a hard time because I was the founder of the Loving Relationships Training and not married, I didn't let it bother me. I knew that I could be a good teacher on the subject of committed relationships whether I had a legal document recognizing my own important relationships or not. Indeed, having gone my own way, I considered my experience all the more valuable.

Occasionally, however, I wondered if I had a phobia about marriage. Eventually, I conceded that perhaps I might, but this was still okay with me. Why did I need to be married? I knew the most important thing was to stay on my path and serve people. And because I knew that I would not have children, why bother to get married?

But the story did not end there, for suppressed fears always surface sooner or later. One day I was shocked to discover the true source of my case with men and marriage. My experience with my father's "leaving," in fact, was only one aspect of my case. What I was *really* hung up on was a deeply suppressed love-hate dependency relationship with *doctors*. I had always considered all doctors male, since in my own experience, they had been.

It still amazes me that it took me so long to figure this one out. Perhaps I had been unwilling or unable to go through the pattern and release it; it would have been too scary and I was not strong enough to survive it at the time. To give up this pattern, I would have to process very deep fears and uncomfortable feelings.

Still, with all my years seeking enlightenment and all my research in the field of relationships, one would think that I would have figured it out sooner. And, indeed, if it had not been for these experiences, I might *never* have figured it out. At any rate, the issue came to a head one day when I had to go to a doctor for a minor in-office procedure related to my sinuses. I made this visit around the time I had also begun to grieve my sister's death. Several hours after the appointment, I had a violent allergic reaction to the antibiotic the doctor prescribed, and I remained ill for days. This confirmed the notion that I'd held since my birth, which was that doctors heal you, but then they hurt you. (The doctors, after all, had not been able to save my dad or my sister, and I felt bitterly let down.)

The extreme reaction to the antibiotic, along with the delayed response to my sister's death, left me in a weakened state. I ended up having to see a series of doctors, something I had avoided at all costs since I had left nursing.

The physical complications, however, turned out to be a blessing in disguise. *When I could no longer run from doctors, I suddenly had to face the fact that I was in love with them.* I'd developed a secret psychological dependence on physicians, even though I was seldom sick and rarely needed them. Underneath my cool and often sometimes distainful pose, I was afraid I'd die if it weren't for doctors—but I didn't trust them, either.

After a fourteen-year career in medicine, working as a nurse, I had a lot of issues I'd never cleaned up with doctors. And having had a sick parent, physicians dominated the world of my childhood. Unaware of this, I suppressed, and ultimately rebelled against, my feeling of dependence on doctors by canceling my medical insurance as an adult. Determined to get along without them, I began to study spiritual self-healing methods.

Unfortunately, although my physical symptoms abated, the original problem was not resolved. Even though I'd made both sensible and risky attempts to ease my ties to doctors, the core issue remained untouched.

Then God gave me a gift and a lesson in the form of a boyfriend who had been a doctor. This man was a yogi, someone much like a guru and much like the local doctor in the small town where I grew up. My new partner seemed to have power over everyone. I was drawn to that kind of power. At the same time, it repelled me.

My emotions and moods seesawed, taking their toll on my relationship. One day I would emanate warmth, love, empathy, and tolerance—the next day I would withdraw with cool disinterest. I grew exhausted from these changes and decided to investigate the reasons for my behavior instead of blaming my mate. I scrupulously observed my feelings and behavior, keeping an eye out for both obvious and subtle patterns. I scoured my memory for any clues that would exlain my actions and decisions and followed up on any leads. Then all at once, after months of searching, the answer become startlingly clear to me. One day I began to see that I was projecting my love-hate relationship with doctors onto my intimate relationships with men. I became convinced that this projection was really getting in the way. On a night in early autumn, I had a dream which confirmed my conviction.

In a vaguely defined schoolroom, a gorgeous, sexy man appears at my side. He is very affectionate and attentive to me. I turn to him and ask, "Where did you come from? Did you just materialize?" He tells me how much he wants to be with me and asks me to meet him after class. I assure him I will come, and he explains where we should meet. But as I exit class, someone jumps me. I am thrown to the ground by a stranger and knocked unconscious. When I come to, I realize I have been taken to a doctor because I needed stitches in my hip (in the exact place where the obstetrician had hit me at birth!) When I look up at the doctor after he completes the surgery, he says to me clearly, "I think you make all this stuff up just so you can be with doctors." "You're right," I reply. At that moment, I realize I have lost the sexy man who had approached me in the beginning. It is too late. I have blown it by creating this drama with doctors. Then I awaken.

In working through my case, I went through other dreams, other fears, other memories. I rebirthed, and finally, after a confusing and often difficult time, I forgave doctors. When Bob, the director of the LRT, urged me to write a completion letter to the medical profession, I did it immediately. It was a deeply emotional experience for me. Just as I finished, the diarrhea I had had for a month stopped. The fear was over. Perhaps it will be of value to you if you are facing a similar challenge. The letter documents the journey I had to make and complete.

Completion Letter to All Doctors

Dear Doctors,

I wish to honor all of you who have ever been in my life. At times I have really needed you. Other times, I was addicted to *thinking* I needed you to survive. I have been in love with you, fascinated with you, resisting you, resenting you, really angry at you.

I have felt that you saved me but then you hurt me. I have felt that you have been wrong for telling people, like my father, that they *must* die; that you have acted as if you were God. I have been angry that you did not save my father. I have been relieved that you kept him alive as long as you did. I have hated you for hurting me at my birth. I have loved you for saving everyone that you saved, especially for caring about people in my same town. I have tried to reject medicine. I have tried to forget you. I have felt sympathy with you for all you went through in medical school.

I have been stuck on you so much that it has prevented me from having perfect relationships with men. I have had relationships I'm not proud of. I have worshipped you. I have felt you have all the power and so I must be with you. I have thought you were gurus. I have believed I could not live without you. I have tried to prove I could live without you by canceling my medical insurance for ten years. Then I came back and tried to forgive you. Then I resisted the urge to forgive you. I transferred my addiction to healers and clairvoyants instead. Then I fell in love with one of you.

When I was a little girl, I was grateful that you made home visits and came to our house to tenderly heal us. I thought you were *always there*. At least someone was *always there for me* when my father was not. I went into nursing so I could be with you. I wanted to be near you and serve you and have your power. I wanted to marry a doctor. Then I decided I would *never* marry a doctor. I hated the fact that you were never at home with your families, that you were always in the hospitals, night and day. I got tired of taking phone calls from your wives begging you to come home. I felt sad seeing you fall asleep over the charts. Later, when I ran away to foreign countries and got married, I could finally stop thinking about you. My husband could be the doctor instead, even though he was not a real doctor.

The funny part of all of this was that *I* myself was almost never even sick! I never really needed much help from you; most of the time I have been a true picture of health. Needing you was only an obsession in my mind. Being well all the time was strange, though, because everyone else was sick. I thought I was supposed to be sick to be "normal." Sometimes I made up things so I could see you. People who were constantly well and totally alive were odd. This left me in a dilemma: I wanted to be like everyone, to be accepted. Yet I wanted to be different at the same time. But the part of me that was *afraid* that someday I might die made me remain dependent on you psychologically.

The way I arranged to see you was by going to dentists instead. I created a lot of cavities, and I fell in love with my dentist. He gave me little plaster-of-paris angels. He treated me like a little queen. If I couldn't be sick, unconsciously I knew that at least I could have contact with the medical profession through him. I almost married a dentist. Then I decided I *never* wanted to marry a dentist—they have the highest suicide rate, and besides, I am not the suburban type.

Once I had to have a minor surgery on my hand and you gave me an anesthesia I was allergic to. I ended up looking like a monster. It was terrifying. Many of the drugs you gave me over the years, I was seriously allergic to and they made me worse. This affirmed my belief that doctors heal you and then they hurt you.

And then five of you took my virginity all at once in an operating room procedure. I cannot even bear to think about the implications of that action. It is something I totally suppressed. Of course, maybe I stopped my periods for thirteen months just so I would have to have that oophorsostomy. There was, of course, nothing wrong with me. There almost never is. I was just shut down due to my father's death. I made up symptoms that could not be diagnosed. I got the rheumatic fever symptoms once but didn't even have spirochetes. I was simply trying to be like my father. Lately, I have tried to be like my sister, to get the diseases she had so she would love me. I have made up all these symptoms to be like others or near you. None of it is real. I didn't go around planning this. It is all unconscious.

I am proud that I have only been in hospitals a couple of times for very minor problems. But I spent a lot of time visiting my father in hospitals. He was always in hospitals with you!

Please forgive me for all my confusion, projections, and anger. Once I really got furious at all of you when I went by the National Institute of Health in Washington, D.C. I rolled down the window and shouted very loudly, *"When are you guys going to get it that thought is creative and negative thoughts are what cause all disease?"*

At medical conferences I have really been disgusted at some of you for not listening to speakers who discussed the metaphysical aspects of healing and for putting down doctors, like Bernie Segal, who have the guts to speak out and use new approaches. Don't we all have to be open to change? So what if we spend fortunes on our medical training? What if some of it was off? Must we defend things that may be off? I felt really upset when some of you put down the doctor at a conference who stood up and confessed that one of the biggest mistakes made in medicine was to put babies in a nursery, away from their mothers, for the convenience of doctors. Some of you were angry at him for his audacity. Why? What if he is right?

What if we *are*, in fact, under no laws but God's? There are people who do *not* need eight hours of sleep. There are people who do not need three meals a day. There are women who *can* take birth control pills after 40 and be okay. Can we be heard? Is it right to reject chiropractics? Is it right to reject homeopathy and ayurvedic medicine or healers that are producing good results, just because they are somehow a threat to the established medical profession? Can't we all work together?

I want to remain on good terms with you. I want to accept you as you are and I notice that is hard because now I feel like trying to change you. I want to appreciate you and support your work. I want to thank you. I want to work with you in a new way to improve health in the world. But what I do not want is the thought that I need you in order to survive. I want to be very clear that I am safe and immortal right now and I can live and keep living whether I have a doctor or not. I am alive by the light of God. I forgive myself for blaming you. I forgive myself for needing you. I forgive myself for being in love with you. I forgive myself and my family for being addicted to you. I forgive myself for being angry at you. Will you forgive me?

Can't we work together and try to understand the real truth about rejuvenation, spiritual healing, and longevity? Will you be open to my books and our research in rebirthing and not reject them just because our findings may be different from the theory in your books? Will you please not knock rebirthing until you try it? Don't we all want the same thing—perfect health for ourselves and everyone, peace, love, and happiness for everyone? I have studied spiritual healing for fifteen years, since I left the nursing profession. I don't want to have to be separate from you just because I have other techniques. I do not want to reject medicine either. Why shouldn't we all work together?

I pray that my relationship with you can now be totally healed and complete and new. Because the real truth is that I have devoted my whole life to trying to understand why people get sick and why people die. It did not make sense to me to be in medicine and try to heal people without understanding the *cause*. Perhaps I have been afraid to speak up on what I have learned because my fears of confronting authority. I know many people who are actually afraid of the American Medical Association. Anyway, I am going to see all doctors and the AMA as loving and dedicated to the truth and willing to be open to all true spiritual knowledge.

So with that I am going to tell you that I actually had the audacity or whatever you want to call it—call it courage—to write a book on physical immortality. I invite you to read the whole book before you reject it. What if giving up the death urge is the *real key* to health? Please don't knock it until you try it. Please try to understand that it is my spiritual mission to put out this information and all I ask is that you respect my attempts to have more life, more joy, and more health for everyone. I will, in turn, respect the part of you that wants the same. Thank you.

Love,
Sondra Ray

Review

1. Develop and cultivate many friendships always.

2. Turn over your special relationship to the Holy Spirit for purification.

3. Get into balance with money: reject greed, but avoid the money rejection complex, also.

4. Clear your resistance to receiving. Understand that substance is the cause and money an effect.

5. Avoid fighting about money. The addiction to conflict is the real cause of money problems.

6. Let go of guilt and remember your innocence.

7. Clean up your life; start with your own house. Throw away what is not of purpose. Fix everything. Make each room sparkling. Go over your wardrobe carefully. Clean up your car, your yard, and the planet.

· PART VII ·

Important Spiritual Matters

Reviewing *A Course in Miracles*

I have decided to include a collection of important teachings from *A Course in Miracles* here because I believe a deep understanding of that work is basic to the quest to right ourselves and our relationships.

When one of my spiritual teachers called the Course the most important written work since the Bible, I was determined to study it meticulously. Having done so, I've come to agree wholeheartedly with my teachers assessment. While appreciating *A Course in Miracles* will prove easy for the reader, describing it is no easy matter. The Course cannot be defined as a path, nor is it a religion. In the end, it may be most accurately described as a *correction*. The text is Christian in tone because Christianity must be corrected first, since it has such a major influence on the industrialized societies which threaten the planet. Whether or not you realize it, by growing up during the era of Western dominance, you were heavily influenced by Christianity—even if you were not raised in the Christian faith.

At the same time, the Course expressly explains that its Christian references represent universal ones:

> *The name of Jesus Christ as such is but a symbol. But it stands for love that is not of this world. It is a symbol that is safely used as a replacement for the many names of all*

the gods to which you pray... This Course has come from him because his words have reached you in a language you can love and understand (manual, p. 55, 56).

The Course contrasts what it calls the "ego's thought system" with the "Holy Spirit's thought system." The ego's thought system has deceived us, having led us to believe that we have separated ourselves from God and that, therefore, God is out to destroy us for this "sin." As a result, we perpetually fear we will be punished. Under these conditions, our body becomes a defense against and a refuge from God.

Fleeing from the realm of the Holy Spirit, we end up with a tremendous fear of God—and so the bargaining begins. We petition for God to be lenient and make him an offer: "You don't have to go to the trouble of punishing me—I will punish myself."

In traditional Judeo-Christian-Islamic theology, the only way to please the so called "wrathful God" is to suffer. This mentality leads directly to the concept of sacrifice: "I will suffer and deprive myself to prove I am good so you won't get too angry, God." Sickness is one of the means by which we castigate ourselves. Pain is another. The ego's thought system fosters the insane notion that sacrifice is salvation: Sacrifice is holy. To suffer is holy. To the ego, God's will for us is perfect misery. We don't deserve to be happy, and the more we suffer now, the better we will be later on. This makes no sense. How then can we have any sort of positive relationship with ourselves or with others under these circumstances? It is impossible.

Genesis chronicles the birth of the ego. When the serpent presses Eve to take the forbidden fruit, promising her she "will be like God," she succumbs to the temptation. *The moment Eve concedes that she needed to do anything to be "like God," she has confirmed that she is separate from God.* By doing so, Eve "fell from the Garden," meaning that she departed from the realm of the Holy Spirit. At the same moment, she entered the realm of the ego, becoming separate, rather than one, with God. In this way, Eve created her own hell, for *"hell is what the ego makes of the present* (text, p. 281)," while heaven is the state of perfect oneness.

The Old Testament is rife with sin, guilt, and punishment. It presents a picture of an angry and vengeful God, and it tells us that eventually we must all perish. The Bible itself is a mixed bag full of egotistical feelings and expressions of love. It sends out the double messages: "I love you," *and* "I will beat the hell out of you"; "God is loving," *and* "His punishment is severe";"God created love and peace," *and* "He also created pain, suffering, and death." These contradictions, like the pairing of heaven and hell, make no sense. If they described a true picture of the world, God would indeed be cruel.

We must rethink our concept of God. When false concepts lie at the center of a thought system, the whole system will be *deceptive*. The lie at the heart of most traditional religious doctrine asserts that human beings are separate from God. Nothing in the universe will make any sense if we buy that line. For, indeed, it is impossible for us to be separate from God.

The traditional interpretation of Jesus's crucifixion that we have inherited has left us extremely confused. This account was in fact borrowed from Isaiah's story, that of the suffering servant. But the mix-up doesn't end there. The traditional version leads us to conclude that only one person has to suffer to save all human beings who are sinners. Let's consider what kind of effect this has on us. How would you feel if you committed a serious mistake or crime, but someone else—completely innocent and entirely good—had to die for it? Furthermore, what sort of effect would it have on you if you had been given such an interpretation since early childhood? Very likely, you would experience overwhelming guilt. Yet salvation is supposed to *free* us from guilt!

Under such a thought system, the Savior's suffering actually serves no purpose, since it reinforces the very thing it is supposed to correct. Instead, human ego twists Jesus's message of love and peace and forgiveness into a gospel of division.

One of Christianity's greatest errors was to portray Jesus as a victim. Because New Testament accounts of Jesus's words and deeds were written down decades, and in some cases more than a *century*, after he died, they do not always represent an accurate distillation of his life and teachings. The authors of the New Testament filtered the gospel through their own egos and guilt, at times promoting the idea that human beings are wretched and only Jesus is "special." Followers such as Paul, for example, preached that we on earth are *not good enough*, rather than hearing the uplifting and forgiving message that Jesus so lovingly and generously offered.

The truth is that Jesus' presence was *so pure* that it was devastating. For his disciples, it brought up their cases totally. They had to obscure the meaning of his life and work in shadows of the past. Subsequently, human beings passed through 2,000 years of what we at LRT call a "response column." "Response column" is any negative reaction you have to an affirmation—any resistance to it or debate about it that would keep you from accepting it. It is any *protest* you invent blocking you from integrating the truth. We say "love brings up anything unlike itself." Because the presence of Jesus was one of total purity, it brought up anything unlike purity, and it stimulated two millennia of ego reaction. Now Jesus has come around again, giving us another chance to get it. He is saying, "Look, I told you 2,000 years ago to seek the Kingdom of Heaven within, I taught you that you and the Father are one, but you did not get it. So I will try again."

The Course says "everything we know is wrong." We must start over, dispensing with our imagined separation from God. (How can a sunbeam exist independently of the sun?) There can be no separation; it is impossible. Sin, therefore, does not exist because every act we commit is connected to the Holy Source (paraphrase, text, p. 364, 365).

It is wise to follow Jesus because he completed himself perfectly and taught liberation. This practice has nothing to do with traditional worship as we know it. Because our identity *is* Spirit, to Jesus, all sins are already forgiven in the Holy Instant. In eternity we are no different than He, because we are all sons of God.

Through the oppressive viewpoint of traditional Christianity, we are victimized by our own bodies, our parents, and nature itself. The Course reveals that there are no victims and that no perception of oneself as a victim is ever justified. This, indeed, is the lesson of the Resurrection. The Crucifixion was an extreme teaching device aimed at the Resurrection. Christ taught that it *is* possible to atone oneself without sacrifice. True atonement means allowing the Holy Spirit to correct all your mistaken thinking.

A Course in Miracles teaches that there exists no world outside us, only a projection of what is inside us. For our personal bodies are a projection of our minds. The only purpose the world or our body serves is to teach us that there is no world or body outside our own perception. The temple of the Holy Spirit manifests itself not in a body, but by using our body lovingly to learn more about love. In this way our goal is to make all our relationships holy.

You must be willing to question every value you ever had (paraphrase, text, p. 464). This is the only way that you can eventually understand that you are *innocent.* Initially, your reactions will seem confusing. You will not believe you deserve to have or maintain a really loving relationship, nor that you deserve success and physical immortality. You will think you are guilty, and guilt may sabotage your attempts to move forward. You may have trouble accepting your innocence if you are obsessed with things you did that you think are "bad."

Ultimately, the important thing to remember is that you *do* have forgiveness in the Holy Instant and that this idea is not entirely alien. Suppose you go into your child's room and you see he is thrashing about having a nightmare. How would you deal with it? Like any loving parent who wants to minimize a child's discomfort, you do not get involved in the dream itself, making the nightmare real. Instead, you turn on the light, call his name and remind him who he is. This, too, is how God cares for us. He is not at all involved in our ego, the entity that makes us do "bad" things. Because he knows we are just asleep in a nightmare, wrestling with the ego, he does not even make those so-called sins real. With his greater perception, he sees our true reality. In this Holy Instant, no one is at fault, and therefore there is nothing to forgive. That is why you are innocent.

(It may be necessary to read the preceeding over several times in order to get the full effect and the consequences of these truths on your relationships.)

Holy vs. Unholy Relationships

We are always encouraging everyone to read the entire *A Course in Miracles* over and over again. This chapter will summarize what the Course's teachings says on the subject of relationships. Though, in fact, the entire Course concerns relationships, I've concentrated on chapters 15, 16, 17, 20, and 22, which discuss the tyranny of the "special relationship." The Course also identifies what it calls the "special hate relationship." It warns us not to be afraid to look at these darker and more difficult relationships, for our freedom rests on our ability to address them (paraphrase, text, p. 313).

As the Course explains, in a special relationship, we regard one individual as more "special" than anyone else, more valuable than ourselves, and even more precious than God. But this idea is a delusion. As children of God, all human beings together comprise the Sonship. In coveting a special relationship with one human being, we limit our love to only one small segment of the Sonship. And somewhere inside of us we are inevitably aware that we have forsaken the totality of the Sonship. This brings guilt into our relationship, and guilt houses fear.

The special love relationship is a compelling distraction we use to obscure our attraction to God the Father. In other words, within the special relationship, we deny our need for God by substituting the need for special people and special things. Hope of salvation depends solely on one individual, and so the attention our partner may devote to activities outside the relationship feels like a threat to our well-being. Because special relationships delude us into believing they can offer salvation, we also accept the erroneous idea that *separation is salvation.* In fact, such exclusive relationships serve as the ego's chief weapon in barring us from a heavenly existence.

An unholy relationship feeds on differences; each partner perceives that his mate possesses qualities or abilities he does not. On the surface, such a partnership seems to bear out the old claim that "opposites attract." Upon closer inspection, however, a different picture emerges. In reality, each partner enters into such a union with the idea of *completing themselves and robbing the other.* They each remain in the relationship only until they decide that there is nothing left to steal, and then they move on.

Within these kinds of relationships, whatever reminds a person of past grievances attracts them. In the Loving Relationships Training we call this "being attracted to your patterns." It's obvious that partners in this kind of relationship are not there out of a wish to join with their mate in Spirit. More surprising, however, is the fact that such people are not even attempting to join with the *body* of their mate. Instead, they seek a union with the bodies of those *who are not there* (paraphrase, text, p. 331)—such as their father or mother or others. Based on unspiritual impulses, this unholy bond has little to do with real love. This attempt at union ultimately excludes the very person with whom the partnership was made (paraphrase, text, p. 321).

The special love relationship also has a flip side. In the special hate relationship, negative impulses are merely more transparent, for the relationship is clearly one of anger and attack. In this arrangement, one person becomes the focus of our anger; we hold on to everything they have done to hurt us. The special hate relationship wreaks vengeance on the past. It holds the past against us (paraphrase, text, p. 323). And it involves a great amount of pain, anxiety, despair, guilt, and attack (paraphrase, text, p. 317).

Every special relationship you have made is a substitute for God's will, and glorifies your own instead. Every special relationship harms you by occupying your mind so completely that you cannot hear the call of Truth.

A special relationship is based on the assumption that something within us is lacking and therefore we have special needs. To satisfy these needs, we come to believe that another individual is capable of giving us that which is missing in ourselves. A conviction of our own littleness lies at the heart of every special relationship, for when two mates endeavor to become one entity, they have forgotten the presence of God in their relationship. Rather than augmenting the relationship, this diminishes its greatness.

In sharp contrast to the special relationship, a "holy relationship" rests on solid ground. Each partner has looked within himself and perceives nothing inherent lacking. Accepting his own completion, he finds pleasure in extending it, and so joins with another person who is also whole. Because they have both evolved to the same degree, no great differences exist between them. This relationship contains and reflects heaven's holiness.

Completion comes from union with God, and from the extension of that union to others. As such, a holy partnership mirrors the rich relationship between the Son of God and his Father; it has the power to alleviate all suffering. In such a partnership, sin cannot exist, since

God himself has arranged each holy union in accordance with His own plan.

A holy relationship requires that both partners strive together toward a common goal. When two people share the same intent and they search for the love of God, a healing takes place. Giving flows endlessly. No wants or needs hinder it, for in giving of themselves, both are blessed. Moreover, these blessings flourish and extend to others. A light emanates outward, illuminating to the world. In a holy relationship, seemingly difficult situations are accepted as blessings. Instead of obsessively criticizing one's partner, forever pointing out any imperfections that must be changed or discarded, there is a pull toward praise and appreciation. Having created an atmosphere of love, each partner may begin to perceive the Christ in each other.

A Course in Miracles on Relationships

The concept of the *Sonship* must be counted as one of the most important ideas presented in *A Course in Miracles*. The Sonship is made up of all God's children, meaning Jesus and all humankind. It's wholeness and integrity provide a solid foundation for world peace:

> *It should especially be noted that God has only one Son. If all His creations are His Sons, every one must be an integral part of the whole Sonship. The Sonship in its oneness transcends the sum of its parts . . . conflict cannot ultimately be resolved until all the parts of the Sonship have returned.* (text, p. 29)

The Course's narrator, presumed to be Jesus, warns us to avoid separation from our brothers. In appreciating one another, we honor the Holy Spirit most deeply:

> *You cannot understand yourself alone. This is because you have no meaning apart from your rightful place in the Sonship, and rightful place of the Sonship is God.* (text, p. 73)

> *Your gratitude to your brother is the only gift I want. I will bring it to God for you, knowing that to know your brother is to know God. If you are grateful to your brother, you are grateful to God for what He created. Through your gratitude you come to know your brother, and one moment of real recognition makes everyone your brother because each of them is of your Father.* (text, p. 63)

Ironically, when crises destabilize our lives—just when we most need each other's support—we often feel a strange inner "pull," separating us from friends and acquaintances. But disassociation is no solution, it is a delusion (paraphrase, text, p. 136). The Course teaches us:

> *Alone we can do nothing, but together our minds fuse into something whose power is far beyond the power of its separate parts.* (text, p. 136)

> *Our function is to work together, because apart from each other we cannot function at all. The whole power of God's Son lies in all of us, but not in any of us alone. . . . Whom God has joined cannot be separated, and God has joined all His Sons with Himself.* (text, p. 139)

> *You cannot enter God's presence . . . alone. . . . All your brothers must enter with you, for until you have accepted them you cannot enter. For you cannot understand Wholeness unless you are whole.* (text, p. 185, 186)

You must recognize your brother as your savior and friend, with whom you will travel to paradise, the "home that called you:"

> *Give joyously to one another the freedom and the strength to lead you there. And come before each other's holy altar where the strength and freedom wait, to offer and receive the bright awareness that leads you home. The lamp is lit in both of you for one another. And by the hands that gave it to your brother shall both of you be led past fear to love.* (text, p. 399)

Only your brother holds the power to forgive your errors. And he, in turn, must seek forgiveness from someone other than *himself*. No one of us can forgive ourselves alone:

> *Beside each of you is one who offers you the chance of Atonement, for the Holy Spirit is in him. Would you hold his sins against him, or accept his gift to you? Is this giver of salvation your friend or enemy? Choose which he is, remembering that you will receive of him according to your choice.*

> *There is no grace of Heaven that you cannot offer to one another, and receive from your most holy Friend. . . . Think who your brother is, before you would condemn him. And offer thanks to God that he is holy. . . . Join him in gladness, and remove all trace of guilt from his disturbed and tortured mind. . . . Give faith to one another for faith and hope and mercy are yours to give. Into the hands that give, the gift is given. . . .* (text, p. 394)

It is not our job, the Course explains, to change our brother, but to accept him as he is, for "his errors do not come from the truth that is him" (text, p. 156). We need to take a good look at where we invest our valuable energy. When we react to our brother's errors as if they are real, we actually *make* them a reality. In confirming that our brother's sins are real, we condemn ourselves—for all of us comprise the Sonship.

When we accept our brother *unconditionally*, on the other hand, we open the door loving all of humanity. Yet acceptance doesn't mean a mere absence of condemnation. For *correction*, however well intended, can also become a form of attack:

> *The choice to judge rather than to know is the cause of the loss of peace. . . . You have no idea of the tremendous release and deep peace that comes from meeting yourself and your brothers totally without judgment. In the presence of knowledge all judgment is automatically suspended. . . .* (text, p. 42)

When you correct a brother you are telling him that he is wrong. He may be making no sense at the time, and it is certain that, if he is speaking from the ego, he will not be making sense. But your task is to still tell him he is right. . . . He is still right, because he is a Son of God. . . . If you point out the errors of your brother's ego you must be seeing through yours, because the Holy Spirit does not perceive his errors . . . nothing the ego makes means anything. . . . When a brother behaves insanely, you can heal him only by perceiving the sanity in him. (text, p. 155)

According to the Course, all conflict arises from the ego, for "only the Holy Spirit is conflict-free" (text, p. 91):

. . . the ego perceives itself at war and therefore in need of allies. You who are not at war must look for brothers and recognize all whom you see as brothers, because only equals are at peace. Because God's equal Sons have everything, they cannot compete. Yet if they perceive any of their brothers as anything other than their perfect equals, the idea of competition has entered their minds. (text, p. 108)

Every response to the ego is a call to war—Those whom you perceive as opponents are part of your peace, which you are giving up by attacking them. . . . When you give up peace, you are excluding yourself from it. (text, p. 128)

Let's consider the major causes of conflict: guilt and blame. Where do these originate? Are they real or imagined? The Course explains that guilt and blame arise from the same source—the ego—and that neither has any place in the realm of the infinite:

The ego tells you all is black with guilt within you, and bids you not to look. Instead, it bids you look upon your brothers, and see the guilt in them. . . . (text, p. 244)

> *If your brothers are part of you and you blame them*
> *for your deprivation, you are blaming yourself. And you*
> *cannot blame yourself without blaming them.* (text, p. 187)

> *If God knows His children as wholly sinless, it is*
> *blasphemous to perceive them as guilty.* (text, p. 178)

The ego expresses itself in both overt and less obvious ways. Though
we may be aware of how the ego drives us to attack or to cause
conflict, we're often "in the dark" when it comes to recognizing the
ego's more insidious role as the mastermind of our *projections*. What
are projections, and how do they work? When we project, we
unconsciously displace all of our *own* feelings—our fears, anger,
love, disgust, disinterest—onto another person. We come to believe
quite sincerely that the *other person really has these feelings, instead*
of ourselves:

> ... *the ego is incapable of trust.* ... *It believes that your*
> *brothers* ... *are out to take God from you. Whenever a*
> *brother attacks another, that is what he believes. Projec-*
> *tion always sees your wishes in others. If you choose to*
> *separate yourself from God, that is what you will think*
> *others are doing to you.* (text, p. 119)

As you know, mistakenly attributing feelings to your partner which
she does not have can only cause havoc in a relationship:

> *The ego cannot tolerate release from the past.* ... *It*
> *dictates your reactions to those you meet in the present*
> *from a past reference point, obscuring the present reality*
> ... *you will then react to your brother as though he were*
> *someone else, and this will surely prevent you from recog-*
> *nizing him as he is [now].* (text, p. 229) ... *To perceive*
> *truly is to* ... *perceive a brother only as you can see him*
> *now. His past has no reality in the present.* (text, p. 233)

Letting go of the past and all projections associated with it is no small
feat. It requires an act of faith—and *faith* is exactly what *A Course in*
Miracles urges us to act upon. Faith, we are told, is the only road to
peace:

> *Believe in your brothers because I believe in you, and you will learn that my belief in you is justified. Believe in me by believing in them, for the sake of what God gave them. Do not ask for blessings without blessing them. . . .* (text, p. 154)

> *When you accepted trust as the goal for your relationship, you became a giver of peace as surely as your Father gave peace to you. For the goal of peace cannot be accepted apart from its conditions. . . .* (text, p. 346)

As all ancient spiritual scriptures attest, we will have to overcome great obstacles along the road to peace. The greatest of these is the ego. As it tries to obscure our path, the ego plays games not only with the mind and the spirit, but also with our flesh. As we travel down this road, we may be pulled in two directions. While the Holy Spirit guides us to use our bodies solely to reach our brothers to *connect* with one another, the ego uses our bodies to *separate* us, by encouraging us to attack our brothers:

> *The Holy Spirit reaches through [the body] to others. You do not perceive your brothers as the Holy Spirit does, because you do not regard bodies solely as a means of joining minds and uniting them with yours and mine. . . . If you use the body for attack, it is harmful to you. . . . Communication ends separation. Attack promotes it.* (text, p. 140)

> *Remember that those who attack are poor.* (text, p. 205) *If you will recognize that all the attack you perceive is in your mind and nowhere else, you will at last have placed its source and where it begins it must end.* (text, p. 207) *You have no enemy except yourself. . . . Beware of the temptation to perceive yourself unfairly treated.* (text, p. 523)

> *The strong do not attack because they see no need to do so. Before the idea of attack can enter your mind, you must have perceived yourself as weak. . . . No longer*

> *perceiving yourself and your brothers as equal, and regarding yourself as weaker, you attempt to "equalize" the situation you made. (*text, p. 209)

But what should we do when another person's actions have harmed us—have we no right to blame him? *A Course in Miracles* answers this question in a surprising way. "When a brother acts insanely," it says, he actually offers us "an opportunity to bless him" (text, p. 118). In this way, his needs lay bare our *own*, for we also *need the blessing we can give* (paraphrase, text, p. 118):

> *There is no way . . . to have it except by giving it. This is the law of God, and it has no exceptions.* (text, p. 118) *We must exempt no one from the love we feel, or we will be hiding a dark place in [our] mind where the Holy Spirit is not welcome.* (text, p. 227)

How far should we go in reaching out to another? What good will it do for us to keep trying, when we see no possible solution to our brother's problem?

> *The Bible says that you should go with a brother twice as far as he asks. Devotion to a brother cannot set you back either. . . . It can lead only to mutual progress. The result of genuine devotion is inspiration, a word which properly understood is the opposite of fatigue.* (text, p. 47)

> *It is impossible to overestimate your brother's value. . . . It will be given you to see your brother's worth when all you want for him is peace. And what you want for him you will receive.* (text, p. 405)

Love's path steadily weaves it's way through every paragraph of *A Course in Miracles*. Without a doubt, the commitment to love is the Course's most precious gift to us, and the text's central theme:

> *Every loving thought is true. Everything else is an appeal for healing and help, regardless of the form it takes. Can anyone be justified in responding with anger to a brother's plea for help? No response can be appropriate*

except the willingness to give it to him, for this and only this is what he is asking for. (text, p. 200)

When you meet anyone, remember that it is a holy encounter. As you see him you will see yourself. As you treat him you will treat yourself. As you think of him, you will think of yourself. Never forget this. . . . Whenever two Sons of God meet, they are given another chance at salvation. (text, p. 132)

Only appreciation is an appropriate response to your brother. Gratitude is due him for both his loving thoughts and his appeal for help, for both are capable of bringing love into your awareness if you perceive them truly. (text, p. 201)

Give them the appreciation God accords them always, because they are His beloved Sons in whom He is well pleased. You cannot be apart from them because you are not apart from Him. . . . You cannot know your own perfection until you have honored all those who were created like you. (text, p. 119)

When your relationships are free of blame, no one can harm you. If your center is intact and your heart with God, you will be able to adjust to even the most sudden and fundamental change.

You cannot be hurt, and do not want to show your brother anything except your wholeness. Show him that he cannot hurt you and hold nothing against him, or you hold it against yourself. This is the meaning of 'turning the other cheek.' (text, p. 75)

Overlooking our brother's errors does not mean going away wounded and resentful. We must not separate ourselves from him. Taking his arm, we must walk together with him. In this way, we become closer to him still:

By following [the Holy Spirit] you are led back to God where you belong, and how can you find the way except by taking your brother with you? . . . You forsake yourself and God if you forsake any of your brothers. You must learn to see them as they are, and understand they belong to God as you do. (text, p. 76)

All my brothers are special. If they believe that they are deprived of anything, their perception becomes distorted. When this occurs the whole family of God or the Sonship is impaired in its relationships. . . . God is not partial. All His children have His total Love, and all His gifts are freely given to everyone alike.

The fact that each one has this power completely is a condition entirely alien to the world's thinking. The world believes that if anyone has everything there is nothing left. (text, p. 41)

Isn't it beautiful that *all* of us *can* really *have everything*—that we can all have our power *completely,* all at the same time? Imagine if everyone in the world understood this! Imagine how it would be if in sharing what we possess we would *lose nothing.* Sharing would simply become an act of love, in no way a threat to our own resources:

The way to recognize your brother is by recognizing the Holy Spirit in him . . . the idea of the Holy Spirit is . . . strengthened by being given away. It increases as you give it to your brother. Your brother does not even have to be aware of the Holy Spirit in himself or in you for this miracle to occur. . . . See him through the Holy Spirit in his mind, and you will recognize Him in yours. What you acknowledge in your brother you are acknowledging in yourself and what you share you strengthen. (text, p. 72)

Nothing real can be increased except by sharing. That is why God created you. (text, p. 64)

The Christ-like voice that dictated *A Course in Miracles* insists that loving our brothers, loving the Holy Spirit, and loving ourselves is *one and the same.* No teaching can be more effective in changing the world:

Recognizing the Majesty of God as your brother is to accept your own inheritance. God gives only equally. If you recognize His gift in anyone, you have acknowledged what He has given you. (text, p. 127)

As you come closer to a brother you approach me, and as you withdraw from him I become distant to you. Salvation is a collaborative venture. It cannot be undertaken successfully by those who disengage themselves from the Sonship, because they are disengaging themselves from me. God will come to you only as you will give Him to your brothers. Learn first of them and you will be ready to hear God. That is because the function of Love is one. (text, p. 63)

Devotions: Worshipping Together as a Couple

To worship means to "revere the worth of" something or someone. Worship is natural, the highest, most nonjudgmental form of love, and to refrain from it is unnatural.

When we worship a person, we see no wrong in him whatsoever. We open ourselves completely to him. If we worship a teacher, we will learn very quickly, for we will be open and receptive to all he has to say. To receive our brother's wisdom, we must pay careful attention to the *way* in which we worship; for discriminatory worship leads us down a meaningless path. Instead, we must worship *all of life* for equality is the only truth. Through worship we gain the most out of life and feel the very best we can. Through worship we contribute to a more advanced civilization.

Once you clarify your own ideas about worship, which may have been muddled by traditional religious perspectives, you can then start over with a new fresh look at worship and devotion. Create your own forms and your own altar honoring your most sacred feelings.

Devotions cleanse our being and bring us nearer to the Holy Spirit. Here are some suggestions for devotions you can do with your partner. They will enhance your relationship and your whole life:

- Breathing together
- Reading *A Course In Miracles* aloud to each other (Try reading it one week in place of the newspapers, which provoke more internal conflict)
- Chanting together
- Meditating together
- Writing affirmations together
- Fasting together
- Appreciating silence together
- Praying together, out loud or in silence
- Fire purification together
- Visiting holy places together
- Listening to spiritual music together
- Shaving your heads at the same time
- Going to a sweat lodge or float-to-relax tank together
- Attending seminars together
- Spreading enlightenment and networking together
- Committing to a Peace Project together

Love

There are many ways to talk about love. In the Loving Relationships Training, we describe love as an omnipresent substance, noticed mostly in the absence of negative thought. According to *A Course In Miracles*, love is beyond definition (paraphrase, text, introduction). In any case, and however we express it, we do know that love is one of the highest energies known to humankind. It can be used to cure physical and mental illness; it can help prolong life. Most of us sense the value of love, and many of us spend a good part of our lives searching for it. Yet it is really not our task to seek love, the Course contends, but to dismantle all the blocks we have built against it (paraphrase, text, p. 315).

In *A Spiritual Approach to Man/Woman Relations*, edited by Scott Miners, we discover that Plato's philosophical explorations into the question of love have been greatly misunderstood. The philosopher did not disparage physical and romantic love between two individuals, as many people think. Instead, he believed that all forms of love are part of an upward pull toward the spiritual, the immortal. He saw love as a ladder consisting of seven steps that ranged from love of an individual to love of the universe's highest realities:

1. Falling in love with the quality of another's form.

2. Loving all beautiful physical form.

3. Loving the beauty of mind, regardless of the physical form.

4. Loving beautiful practices such as ethics, fairness, justice, kindness.

5. Developing a love of beautiful institutions—family, society, holistic feeling, and so on.

6. Developing a love of the universal and abstract, including the sciences. Loving the whole cosmos, harmony and order, and laws of the universe.

7. Experiencing love of the everlasting manifestation of beauty itself, the Absolute.

For Plato, love and beauty were inextricably connected. Physical love was the first step in a progression that led to falling in love with the whole universe. The final step unites us with the Infinite Source of Being and immortality. Self-transcendence is the high point of the greater mysteries of love.

Physical Immortality

I know of nothing that will revitalize a relationship like the goal of physical immortality. Most people feel unsettled by the idea of living forever, and the concept may even strike them as "anti-spiritual," since it differs so markedly from traditional church doctrine. Nothing could be farther from the truth. Life is sacred. When you choose more life, you become holier. Such a choice is absolutely spiritual.

In my recently published book *How to Be Chic, Fabulous, and Live Forever*, I discuss physical immortality at length. The title was deliberately chosen to wake up readers and to make it fashionable to think about and discuss immortality. Other immortalists, such as Anna Lee Skarin, are also breaking ground in this debate. Skarin, an Immortal Master who can dematerialize and rematerialize at will, champions the sacred gift of life in her book, *The Celestial Song of Creation* (she is also the author of *Beyond Mortal Boundaries*):

> *Death itself begins with the cells and the tissues as they are gradually undermined and destroyed by the vibrations of all negative evil thoughts and fears. Death comes because the individual himself relinquishes the gift of life. He permits the life force to be crowded out by his own tired, resentful, self-pitying thoughts; his negative attitudes, degenerative desires and greedy actions. Every discordant negative word and attitude are but destructive forces of death bombarding the life of man. The life principle is gradually crowded out and defeated by man's ignorance.*

The gift of life is exalted and increased through joy, right thinking, and the positive force of right action. Skarin goes on to explain that as the sacred life force increases, old age and physical deterioration ends. They are conquered as the cells of the body are spiritualized and released from death. This is what the Bible calls "overcoming"— death is automatically conquered through the exaltation of love, praise, and gratitude.

Remember that every individual resides within the vibrations of his own thoughts and mental habits. Vibrations of ecstasy and inner praise nurture the vibration of light. We may choose life over death at any time.

What might be blocking you from making this choice? If you knew you could live forever in your physical body without dying, would you be pleased? If not, your life probably matches one of the following descriptions:

- you're neither enjoying daily existence, nor "winning" at the game of life

- your daily life is fine, yet you still believe there is a "higher place"

If you fall into the first category, you'll ask, "Why would I want to live forever when I am not even feeling good now?" A very good question, and yet its answer reveals a paradox: The only way to feel *really* good is to give up the death urge, to begin to truly love life so much that you would be thrilled at the idea of living forever! This is one of the most important secrets of being happy and healthy.

If you fall into the second category—you're doing well enough, but are waiting for a glorious hereafter—imagine how much *more* spectacular life might be if you stop clinging to the belief that somewhere else is better. Death is no solution; it does not necessarily take you to a higher place once you've released your body. As Ruby Nelson tells us in *The Door of Everything*:

> When one chooses to die, death does release the weight of gravity and temporarily frees the soul from earth. But it does not change the vibration of consciousness from the human level. There is no escape from the vibration of yourself except through practiced change of thoughts. Nor does death cause the released consciousness to go to a celestial level. Consciousness, when departing from the body, automatically seeks its own level.

> Every lifetime is a new opportunity to be enlightened and anointed with the light and to rise above the trap of death. For he that is joined to Him that is immortal, will also himself become Immortal.

Notice that Ruby Nelson talks about *choosing* to die. This issue is the key: our belief systems determine our reality. What we believe to be true, we create. Though we've been led to believe otherwise, death is a *choice*. Death is therefore optional.

We must become aware of how the death urge, evident in any anti-life thought, pervades every aspect of our life. The fact that our body may feel perfectly healthy right now does not necessarily mean we have "handled" physical immortality. Our death urge may very well be suppressed, or we may be acting it out in other areas of our life. Ultimately, this destructive urge is the root cause of anything "out there" in your life that is not working. It is supported by the following actions and thought patterns:

- Invalidation of personal divinity
- Lack of immortalist philosophy
- Belief systems fostering disease
- False religious doctrine
- Family tradition
- Overeating and other addictions
- Unresolved tension and birth trauma

The death urge saps vitality and impairs our judgment. We see this destructive impulse surfacing in many aspects of our society. Observing this phenomenon, my friend Leonard Orr has pointed out the danger inherent in electing old men—whose proximity to death heightens their paranoia—to political office. When the death urge dominates a personality, it blocks out wisdom and inhibits creativity.

War itself is the most obvious and destructive manifestation of the death urge, and dismantling our pro-death mentality will be the key to a succesful, lasting peace movement. Disarmament movements that underestimate the effects of this mentality will last only temporarily. Those that unravel the birth/death cycle will endure, contributing to a *solution* to our greatest social and political problems.

Truly, the fusion of body and spirit united in service creates peace. And because Spirit cannot be destroyed, we, too, cannot be stopped if we keep a clear mind and refuse to indulge in ideologies of separation. The traditional path encouraged us to achieve peace and resolve conflicts, whether personal and global, through control and manipulation. Clearly, this method has proven disastrous. Only out of negotiation and understanding will a new way reveal itself and remove fear from our consciousness.

Some critics say that the idea of physical immortality constitutes ultimate self-aggrandizement. Quite frankly, if immortalists were merely striving to live out an endless, purposeless existence I would agree with them. But this is not the case. The real passion for immortality grows out of a selfless dedication to divine service. As one proponent described it, physical immortality is "a condition of maximum efficiency for achieving the true goal of assisting in the world of creation."

Robert Coon, my consultant on this subject, believes that we must take a vow dedicating our will to the attainment of physical immortality. This vow includes a commitment to living fully; it means not letting anything come between us and our spirituality and consciously letting go of our false religious beliefs. We must dispense with the myth that we are separate from God, that we die and go to Heaven and that God determines when we should die.

In my books I have mentioned that aging is controlled by consciousness. Astrologer Linda Goodman's adage, "No anger, no rage, no age!" neatly expresses this concept. She also talks about the body being a self-regenerating battery. There is no way to exaggerate the importance of knowing that this is the truth. You can't just *believe* in it—such ideas lie beyond all belief systems. You have to know it in your bones.

Once you have relinquished your negative religious programming and committed yourself to living fully, you should communicate the truth of everlasting life in your own creative way. You yourself can help resurrect our universe from death.

It is valuable to learn the wisdom of immortals on all of the subjects they write and talk about. Study Linda Goodman's steps toward physical immortality and please take note of the books on this subject that are listed in the bibliography. Before closing, I want to share this wonderful piece by Haridas Chaudhuri, from his book *Being, Evolution and Immortality:*

Physical Immortality:
The Ultimate Phase of Initiation

Finally, the concept of immortality implies a harmonization of the entire personality and a transformation of the physical organism as an effective channel of expression of higher values. This may be called material immortality (rupaniar mukti).

There are some mystics and spiritual seekers who strengthen and purify their bodies just enough to be able to experience the thrilling touch of the Divine. They use the body as a ladder, which by climbing, the pure spiritual level—the domain of immortality—is to be reached. On attaining that level, the body is felt as a burden, as a prison house, as a string of chains that holds one in bondage. Dissociation from this last burden of the body is considered a sine qua non for complete liberation. Continued association with the body is believed to be the result of the last lingering trace of ignorance (avidya leia). When the residual trace of ignorance is gone, the spirit is finally set free from the shackles of the body.

The above view is based upon a subtle misconception about the purpose of life and the significance of the body. The body is not only a ladder that leads to the realm of immortality, but also an excellent instrument for expressing the glory of immortality in life and society. It is capable of being thoroughly penetrated by the light of the spirit. It is capable of being transformed into what has been called the "Diamond Body." As a result of such transformation, the body does not appear any more to be a burden upon the liberated self. On the contrary, it becomes a perfect image of the self. It shines as the Spirit made flesh. It functions as a very effective instrument for creative action and realization of higher values in the world. It is purged of all inner tension and conflict. It is liberated from the anxiety of repressed wishes. It is also liberated from the dangerous grip of the death impulse born of self-repression. Mystics who look upon the body as a burden suffer from the anxiety of self-repression and the allurement of the death wish.

Material immortality means decisive victory over both of these demons. It conquers the latent death instinct in man, and fortifies the will to live as long as necessary, as a channel of expression of the Divine. It also liquidates all forms of self-suppression and self-torture and self-mutilation. As a result the total being of an individual becomes strong and steady, whole and healthy. There is a free flow of psychic energy. It is increasingly channeled into ways of meaningful self-expression. Under the guidance of the indwelling light of the eternal, it produces increasing manifestation of the spirit in matter.

Review

1. Let go of separation—give up specialness. Accept your completion; join with another who is whole!

2. Place your relationship under the care of the Holy Spirit; offer it to be used for His purposes alone.

3. Have a common goal with your mate, such as love of God, or sharing light with the world.

4. Recognize the Holy Spirit in all brothers. Perceive your brothers as equals. Give them only honor and appreciation. Never forget the debt that you owe any brother is gratitude.

5. Give up judgments. Know how to give helpful, supportive feedback as opposed to criticism. Accept your brother as he is, overlooking errors.

6. Sharing and extending to others helps you remember who you are.

7. When you meet anyone, remember that it is a Holy encounter. Accept trust as a goal of your relationship. Give faith to each other.

8. Remember that the purpose of your body's existence is for communication.

9. Respond to pleas for help. Offer your brother release from his ego.

10. In your own way, make it a daily habit of doing devotions and worship together.

11. Make a vow to dedicate your true will to the attainment of physical immortality.

12. Communicate the truth of everlasting life in your own creative way to others.

13. Remember that your true purpose is of selfless dedication to a mission of divine service.

14. Remember that peace comes from fusion of the body and spirit united in service.

15. Bear in mind that the key is living fully, letting nothing come between you and your spirituality.

· PART VIII ·

Committing To the New Age

Committing Your Relationship to the New Age

Today, thousands of us are pledging our relationships to a better future. I can imagine no evolutionary movement more worthy of that commitment than the New Age. Properly understood, the New Age represents a sacred ideal, an *aspect of the Holy Spirit.* My colleague David Spangler underscores this idea when he calls the New Age "a diamond with many facets" and explains that Jesus himself sowed the seeds for this exciting new era.

Yet too often the New Age movement has been presented in a very shallow way, or understood on only a very superficial level. You may well have heard about the more visible manifestations of the New Age movement: crystals and herbs, pyramid power, and the otherworldly intrigue of UFOs. But if you are fortunate, you've also come in contact with a deeper level of exploration: the *transformational* level. Here the New Age has a more important significance as an era of far-reaching spiritual change in the universe.

David Spangler believes that the birth of a new consciousness has heightened the spiritual effect of the New Age, giving us a new awareness of life itself. Under its influence, we adopt a different view of the universe: All is sacred. We also develop a positive image of the future. The mystical aspect of New Age consciousness reaffirms that miracles occur, and the holistic aspect confirms that everything on earth is dependent on everything else. Breaking through borders, the global aspect shows us that as human beings, we actually have more *in common* with than *at odds* with other people on the planet.

The New Age is all about *action*, and seeing our role as *service*. The movement is the vanguard of evolution. As human beings committed to the New Age ideal, we must spiritualize the earth and become warriors against darkness. In doing so, we are swept up in a tidal wave of irresistible growth. We become architects of change, transforming the planet. For more information on David Spangler, read the chapter on him in my book, *Inner Communication*.

Relationships of the Future

It is exciting to think about the relationships of the future and important to have a vision of what they might be like. Resolutely, we must turn to the Creator and ask for guidance in forming such a vision. We must ask for God's intelligence to enter our relationships and our lives, and with that, we can begin.

When I envision the future, I like to imagine individuals becoming totally alive, safe, peaceful, innocent, and present, experiencing their own magnificence. They would be conscious of themselves as expressions of God, remembering their purpose as servers and caretakers of the planet. These "superbeings" would maintain excellent health and would be able to prevent aging and death in themselves. Their lives and efforts would yield a natural abundance and, naturally, they would have a very good time living! These individuals would mate with others like themselves, expressing their Christ nature in a holy relationship that would be totally caring and giving and unselfish. The combined energy of two such people would be extremely exciting and highly productive. Being in the presence of this kind of couple would be tremendously uplifting. The couple would work together with groups on important planetary issues and would be very involved both with local and global communities worldwide. Wherever such individuals appeared and interacted, a tremendous surge of creativity and celebration would flourish.

Futurist visionary Barbara Marx Hubbard, an international champion of social evolution, talks about what she calls a "Supra Sex Revolution." In such a movement, highly evolved beings join together with other like beings in offering their work, acts, and gifts to the world. In doing so, these enlightened people evolve along with society. They become driven to find their "teammates" on this planet with whom they "co-create." This co-creation is so stimulating that it actually produces what Barbara calls "vocational arousal!" In other words, one mate's creativity calls forth their partner's creativity, which reactivates the first mate's creative energy, and so on. We will move into regeneration and rejuvenation and much longer lives. Barbara is currently writing an entire book on the Supra Sex Revolution. We can only look forward to learning more from this incredible visionary!

Review

1. Be part of the Love Corps (a team or group like the Ohana which derives its strength from the quality and balance in relationships of its members).

2. Know that by bonding with others you can have greater stability and pull in higher energies.

3. Become part of the vanguard for humanitarian evolution, always honoring the sacredness of life.

4. Become a superbeing!

Afterword

Closing the Circle

In closing, let's turn once again to a discussion of *purpose*, and a whole way of life which places primary importance on our spirituality. One's relationship should always be seen in the context of that higher goal. Our ideals give us something to refer to and focus on when making our daily decisions and choices. If we can remember our purpose each day, all the elements of our life will hang together in a meaningful way.

What have the mystics taught us about purpose? In his book *The Supreme Ambition*, spiritualist Eknath Easwaran writes that the fulfillment of life's purpose is self-realization, which he likens to a "Sea of Joy, that which we call God." Easwaran, like so many masters, tells us that the "personal discovery that we are all one and indivisible in God" must be our ultimate life. The Saints, he reminds

173

us, have confirmed that life has but one overriding purpose: to discover the Source of Infinite Love, and then to express this love in daily living. Easwaran makes our choices clear: we can struggle through millions of years of dying and reincarnation to reach the Divine, or we can take responsibility for our own evolution by turning inward to discover the source of meaning.

In *The Supreme Ambition*, he carefully describes his own techniques and customs of meditation and prayer which derive from various spiritual traditions. The purpose of meditation, he asserts, is *samadhi*, or union with God. Easwaran advises us to meditate on the prayer of St. Francis of Assisi, "Lord make me an instrument of thy peace. . . ." The person who attains *samadhi*, Easwaran tells us, has simply discovered who he is. Having done so, this person has but one purpose—to help others discover who they are.

Easwaran warns us against spending too much of our life in pursuit of money and material possessions, pleasure, and prestige. There is a danger of becoming so fixated on our own personal wealth that we can easily lose any concern for the welfare of others. He explains that each person has two roads to choose between. A person who takes the first road lives only for herself, her own enjoyment, and satisfaction. During hard times, she clings to what she has, defending it, if she must, against the needs of others. On the other hand, the person who takes the second road chooses what is best for the whole world, of which he is but one small part. In doing so, he has opted for the path of love.

We must, Eknath Easwaran says, see life as one indivisible whole. We must overcome our own individual conditioning and renounce the "I" which separates us from the rest of the world. Perhaps this is what Mahatma Gandhi meant when he said that his greatest ambition was to reduce himself to zero (no ego)—and that it is not possible to be completely happy unless everyone in the world is happy.

With these thoughts in mind, try asking yourself each day: "How much can I give today?" rather than "How much can I make today?" Human beings hunger for power, yet many have forgotten what real power is. Whereas most people are interested in material power, the *rishis*, or great sages, are interested in the power of awareness, or conscious enlightenment. Rejecting materialism, they believe that *real* power lies closer to the Source. When a person can distinguish between authentic and false power, when he knows the spiritual power of love, safety, and certainty, he is following the path of the *rishis*, and will gain true abundance in the process.

Swedish statesman Dag Hammarskjöld once said: "Spirituality is the highest of all human needs and virtues; and the ultimate fulfillment of the human person. Only spirituality will bring peace and justice." Once we truly honor the spiritual life within us, we recover from boredom, ill health, insecurity, and unhappiness. Our personal love relationship ought not to be made a substitute for a healthy spiritual life. Instead, we must immerse our relationships in the richness of our spirituality.

Within Western society, many of us have become disenchanted with the notion of a spirituality because of the so-called spiritual life our parents led. Church sermons were often hypocritical, the beautiful words rarely matched by fine deeds, and the faith seemed largely ineffectual in preventing illness, unhappiness, divorce, or death. When I speak about spiritual life, I am *not* returning to the kind of examples you have observed in the past. I am talking about a very passionate experience that arises within you when your mind is pure, when you break free of the ego. It happens when you remember who you are, when you shed your conditioning and live in the present. It happens in deep meditation, when you really put your full energy into the rebirthing process, or when you do other purification techniques. It happens when you truly want to *live*.

The basic principles of all great religions remain to be an important treasury of power and truth. They teach us universal wisdom:

- All life, the entire phenomenal world, is grounded in a Source that is completely divine.

- Every human being can know this sacred foundation of life.

- Life has only one purpose, to know and experience being united with a sacred presence that we call "God."

You must never lose sight of the Divine Essence; it is the core of your being. You mustn't let anything knock you off center. If you follow these ground rules, you will experience a kind of continuous joy that is not dependent on external occurrences. With such a solid grounding, imagine how much better you could handle relationships! You would be fine even if a relationship ended or changed form. You would simply move on to the next step in life without sacrificing your happiness. Babaji used to say to us, "Be not concerned with praise or abuse. Do your work."

In closing, I ask you to honestly consider these questions:

- Are you clear on your purpose in life now?

- Are you willing to become all that you can become?

- Are you willing to take your own evolution in your hands and get enlightened?

- Are you making spiritual enlightenment a top priority?

- Are you doing all that you can do to support your own well-being and that of others?

- Do you really want to live? Are you constantly strengthening your life urge?

- Are you willing to do all that it takes to stay clear?

- Are you serving humanity?

- Do you now have, or are you willing to have, a mate in the future who is equally committed to this goal?

Loving relationships depend on two people, both willing to experience their own perfection. As Babaji has said, "We are custodians here on earth and we have a duty. We must assist all life-forms to a state of greater development and well-being. Service to others is our main duty."

I hope you will come and join us in the LRT family so we can work toward this goal together. Having you with us would be very exciting.

OM NAMAHA SHIVAI!

Sondra Ray

Appendix

About *Loving Relationships*

The first volume in this series, *Loving Relationships I,* lays the foundations for the ideas covered in this book. *One* helps us gain deep insights into our relationships with lovers, parents, friends, children, bosses, and ourselves. Guiding us toward an understanding of why our relationships turn out as they do, *One* enables us to improve all our relationships.

Although the mechanics of a successful relationship may be *understood* easily enough, maintenance is infinitely more difficult. *Loving Relationships I* pays particular attention to finding, achieving, and maintaining a deeper, more fulfilling relationship with our mate. The author takes us through the depths of self-awareness to a new positive self-image.

Loving Relationships I covers such varied subjects as personal enlightenment, the use of affirmations, rebirthing, loving ourselves and our body, cleaning up destructive behavioral patterns, handling old relationships, and more. Personal accounts of the Loving Rela-

179

tionships Training and profiles of LRT trainers and immortalists complete this book.

I once read a study by Hazelton Clinic. They claimed that there were 5 "common" stages of relationships:

STAGE I   DREAM WORLD   (lasts 6 weeks to 6 months)
STAGE II   DISILLUSIONMENT STAGE   (lasts up to 2 years)
STAGE III   MISERY STAGE   (lasts 6 weeks to 30 years!)
STAGE IV   ENLIGHTENMENT
STAGE V   MUTUAL RESPECT

I was shocked by this. It seemed that by the time you got to the last 2 stages you'd be too old to enjoy them.

What we are trying to do in the LRT is save you 30 years of misery. We want to help everyone get out of disillusionment fast and on to enlightment.

Our centers are listed in the back.

Reports from LRT Graduates

What do people really get out of the Loving Relationships Training? Here are some answers to that question from letters written to us by LRT graduates:

"The feeling that life is worth living—forever."

"Finding a way in which I can handle every single aspect of my life."

"Through the LRT, I have reconnected with God and I can feel that connection."

"I have attracted my ideal loving relationship and it's wonderful."

"I found a workable path toward enlightenment."

"I have learned to manifest my desires quickly! It is a miracle to have a 'world family' like this."

"I was easily and effortlessly able to end a very destructive relationship that had been dragging on for years."

"I got off the habit of relating to women as non-persons, as sex objects who cooked and cleaned and with whom you had sex once a week. I created the gift of being able to share my life with a wonderful, equal woman."

"I was able to understand and have the tools to deal with a block I had about having children of my own."

"I shifted from a life-long pattern of only being able to talk to one or two people at a time, hiding in a corner at parties, to being able to fully engage myself in a leadership role with regular public speaking."

"I was able to resolve my relationship with my daughters, one of whom did not talk to me for a year! I am also more and more alive!"

"I healed my relationship with God."

"I learned to forgive my parents and myself."

"I had a tremendous increase in my prosperity consciousness. My income has increased by 150% since taking the LRT."

"It is a miracle for me to be part of this bonded international community which is dedicated to common goals and spiritual growth."

"I have received the miracle of being in a relationship with a beautiful, sexy, enlightened man who always tells the truth, who is always willing to handle his case, and who supports me in handling mine."

The results are similar all over the world. Here are some examples from LRT graduates in Europe who have written about the gains they have achieved through the Loving Relationships Training:

"A feeling of 'well being.'"

"The power to overcome death."

"Connection with my essence."

"Prosperity in my work."

"Creation of the perfect partner."

"Discovery of universal love."

"Healing of separation."

"Confidence in myself."

"Clearing with the people I live with."

"Learning to receive."

"The joy of being in a family again."

It is one thing to read a book. It is another thing to change your life. If you are inspired by the contents of this book and would like to experience the maximum opportunity for a radiant new life, you have the opportunity to do so by participating in a Loving Relationships Training (LRT) near you.

The following are area contacts. In the event that these contacts have changed by the time you try to reach them, please call (888) 285-6762.

LOCAL CONTACTS

Northeast Region

Jordan Hovey
203-266-0423
212-873-1908

Christa Rivelli
518-453-9252

Jeanie Loomis
203-481-6091

Arne Rantzen
203-264-4217

Barbara Johnson
212-889-5813

Maria Ruiz
617-666-3920

Middle Atlantic Region
Lea Adler
908-495-4838

Valerie McCabe
908-291-1488

Tony LoMastro
215-424-4444

Dean Hochman
410-542-6892

Midwest
Jim Parker
517-694-3662

Shelagh Keleyhers
402-551-0795

South
Jeffrey Baker
404-977-3043

Debi Miller
404-299-1575

West
Peter and Dana Delong
310-545-5405

England
Diana Roberts
(44) (71) 834-6641

Ben Renshaw
(44) (71) 223-0218

Spain
Adolfo Dominguez
Carmen Enguita
(34) (1) 542-1961

France
Patrice Elleguain
Beatrice Santos
(33) (1) 43 59 53 03

Germany
Bernd Schroeder
(49) (30) 785-4196

Ireland
Patsy Brennan
(353) (12) 841-660

Poland
Krystyna Cwartosz
(48) 41 25 330

Sweden
Lars Eric Bergman
(46) (8) 31 40 63

Norway
Solveig Arntsen
(47) (2) 50 85 52

Australia
Maggie Claxton
(61) (75) 922-247

Bibliography

Bibliography

A Course in Miracles (Glen Ellen, CA: Foundation for Inner Peace, 1975)

A Spiritual Approach to Male/Female Relations edited by Scott Miners (Wheaton, IL: Theosophical Publishing House, 1984)

Being, Evolution and Immortality by D.H. Chaudhuri (Wheaton, IL: Theosophical Publishing House, 1974)

Birth and Relationships by Sondra Ray and Bob Mandel (Berkeley, CA: Celestial Arts, 1987)

Door of Everything by Ruby Nelson (Marina Del Rey, CA: De Vorss and Company, 1963)

Drinking the Divine by Sondra Ray (Berkeley, CA: Celestial Arts, 1984)

Escape from Intimacy: Understanding Addictions to Sex, Love and Romance, Relationships by Anne Wilson Schaef (San Francisco, CA: Harper San Francisco, 1989)

How To Be Chic, Fabulous and Live Forever by Sondra Ray (Berkeley, CA: Celestial Arts, 1990)

How to Raise a Child of God by Tara Singh, 2nd ed. (Los Angeles, CA: Life Action Press, 1987)

How to Spiritualize Your Marriage by Swami Kriyananda, 2nd ed. (Nevada City, CA: Crystal Clarity, 1982)

Ideal Birth by Sondra Ray (Berkeley, CA: Celestial Arts, 1985)

I Deserve Love by Sondra Ray (Berkeley, CA: Celestial Arts, 1976)

Journey Without Distance by Robert Skutch (Berkeley, CA: Celestial Arts, 1984)

Linda Goodman's Star Signs by Linda Goodman (New York: St. Martin's Press, 1987)

Love, Medicine and Miracles by Bernie Siegel, M.D. (New York: Harper and Row, 1988)

Loving Relationships I by Sondra Ray (Berkeley, CA: Celestial Arts, 1980)

New Age Tantra Yoga: The Sexual Gateway to Spiritual Fulfillment by Howard J. Zitko (Arizona: World University, 1985)

New Teachings for an Awakening Humanity edited by Virginia Essene (SEE Publishing, 1986)

Other Lives, Other Selves by Roger Woolger (New York: Bantam, 1988)

Peace, Love and Healing by Bernie Siegel, M.D. (New York: Harper and Row, 1989)

Private Lies: Infidelity and the Betrayal of Intimacy by Dr. Frank Pittman (New York: Norton, 1987)

Private Lives: Infidelity and the Betrayal of Intimacy by Frank Pittman (New York, Norton, 1990)

Pure Joy by Sondra Ray (Berkeley, CA: Celestial Arts, 1988)

Quantum Healing: Exploring the Frontiers of Body, Mind and Medicine by Deepak Chopra, M.D. (New York: Bantam, 1989)

Sexual Evolution by Rhonda Levand (Berkeley, CA: Celestial Arts, 1991)

Surfers of the Zuvuya by Jose Arguelles (Santa Fe, NM: Bear & Company, 1988)

Tantra: The Art of Conscious Loving by Charles and Caroline Muir (San Francisco, CA: Mercury House, Inc., 1989)

The Abundance Book by John R. Price (Boerne, TX: Quartus Books, 1987)

The Celestial Song of Children by Annalee Skarin (Marina Del Ray, CA: De Vorss and Company, 1962)

The Esoteric Philosophy of Love and Marriage: The Problem of Purity by Dion Fortune (Great Britain: Thorsons, 1987)

The Only Diet There Is by Sondra Ray (Berkeley, CA: Celestial Arts, 1981)

The Starseed Transmissions by Ken Carey (San Francisco, CA: Harper San Francisco, 1988)

The Supreme Ambition by Eknath Easwaran (Tomales, CA: Nilgiri Press, 1982)

When Society Becomes an Addict by Anne Wilson Schaef (San Francisco, CA: Harper San Francisco, 1987)

Audio Tapes

Return to Love by Marianne Williamson (New York: Harper Audio, 1992)

Spiritual Marriage: an informal talk by Brother Anandamoy on the teachings of Paramahansa Yogananda (Boulder, CO: Self-Realization Fellowship)

Magazine Articles Used in this Text

"The Human Aura" by Bob Tillett. *Intent* vol. 1, no. 3 (Australia)